# Surah Al-Fâtihah

Explained

In The Language Of

**MUSLIM SAINTS AND SCHOLARS**

**PEARLS OF WISDOM**

**Selection by**
**Board of Editors**

**ISBN: 978-09766972-7-5**
**Islam in America Series # 1**

Islam in America Series is a non-sectarian, non-profit literary publications working for the promotion of peace through interfaith dialog and understanding among the religions of the world.

Funds generated from the dissemination of this book will be reinvested in further publications of Islam in America Series.



1st Edition - 2014

PeaceVille Inc.
Delaware, USA

peacevilleusa@hotmail.com

Printed in the P. R. China

# Table of Contents

## PLACE AND TIME OF REVELATION

*Surah Al-Fâtiḫah* was revealed at *Makkah* and is one of the earliest revelations of the Holy Qur'ân.

*(7 verses, 29 words, 139 letters)*

According to some reports *Surah Al-Fâtiḫah* was also revealed a second time at Madînah*. Scholars have documented various reasons for the *Surah* to be revealed more than once. Some of those reasons are: As a reminder; Due to the recurrence of the need; and to illustrate the honor and significance. [1], [2]

---

1 *Imâm Ibne Qayyim, Madarijus Salikeen*
2 *Al-Itqaan fi Uloomul Qur'an of Allaamah Suyuti*

# سورة الفاتحة

## Names of Surah *Al-Fâtihah*

***Al-Fâtihahtal-kitâb* الفاتحة الكتاب** ("The Opening of the Divine Writ")**:** The Surah *Al-Fâtihah* has many titles. The first of these is *Al-Fâtihah-tal-kitab*. It has been given this name because the Holy Qur'ân opens with it. Every Prayer service, supplicating the all Mighty God, Allâh starts with it. It is so called because Allâh, the Supreme, has made it an 'index' for the Qur'ân; and all the verities and spiritual insights set out in the Qur'ân by Allâh, are embedded in it and it comprehends all that people needs to know concerning their origin and their end *(life here and in the hereafter)*.

***Ummul Qur'ân* أم القرآن (Mother of the Qur'ân):** *Al-Fâtihah* has also been named *Ummul Qur'ân* (Mother of the Qur'ân), for it comprehends the totality of the meaning of the Qur'ân in an excellent manner. It has embedded in it all the gems and pearls of the Qur'ân. This Surah is, as it were, a nest for the birds of spiritual knowledge and understanding.

"It teaches us the perfect Prayer. For if we can pray aright, it means That we have some knowledge of Allah And His attributes, of His relations To us and His creation, which includes Ourselves; that we glimpse the source From which we come, and that final goal Which is our spiritual destiny

Under Allâh's true judgment: then We offer ourselves to Allâh and seek His light.

Prayer is the heart of Religion and Faith. But how shall we pray? What words shall convey the yearnings of our miserable ignorant hearts To the Knower of all? Is it worthy of Him or of our spiritual nature to ask For vanities, or even for such physical needs As our daily bread? The Inspired One taught us a Prayer that sums up our faith, our hope, and our aspiration in things that matter. We think in devotion of Allah's name and His Nature; we praise Him for His creation and His Cherishing care; We call to mind the Realities, seen and unseen; We offer Him worship and ask His guidance; And we know the straight from the crooked path By the light of His grace that illumines the righteous."[3]

***Ummul-Kitâb* أم الكتاب (Mother of the Book):** The Surah is also named *Ummul-kitâb*, (Mother of the Book), for it contains the essence of all the teachings of the Noble Qur'ân. The Qur'ân comprises guidance in respect of four sciences; the science of the origin of life, the science of eschatology, the science of Prophethood and the science of the Unity of the Divine Being and His attributes. There is not the least doubt that all these four are comprised in this Surah *Al-Fâtihah.*

It bears this title also on account of the fullness of its teachings concerning all that relates to the spirit. Indeed a seeker cannot achieve his goal until his/her heart is saturated with the realization of the majesty of the Divine and the utter humility of His creatures. For this purpose there is no other 'guide' comparable to this great Surah.

[3] *The Meaning of the Holy Qur'ân by 'Abdullah Yûsuf 'Alî, Tenth Edition. (page 15).*

This Surah derives this title also from its comprehensive approach to the needs of human nature and its indication of all the yearnings of human temperament whether in the domain of human effort or in that of Divine grace. For a human, is in need of' knowledge of the Divine Being and Divine attributes and Divine works for the perfect development of his soul.
He also desires to gain knowledge of Allâh's will and pleasure through the media of His commands, the significance of which is disclosed only through His words. His spiritual urge demands that he should be led by the hand by Divine beneficence and should acquire through this means inner purity and light and Divine communion. This noble Surah *Al-Fâti<u>h</u>ah* encompasses all these objectives. In truth, it charms the hearts with the beauty of its style and the power of its exposition. According to Imâm Bukhari, the designation *Umm al-Kitâb* was given to it by the Holy Prophet himself.[4]

***Al-<u>H</u>amd* الحمد (the Perfect and True Praise and Glory):** Another title is *Al-<u>H</u>amd* (The Perfect and True Praise and Glory), since it opens with the praise and glory of our God Most High. Consider how it proclaims His Majesty and His Greatness beginning with: 'All worthiness of perfect and true praise and glory belongs to Allâh alone, *Rabb* (Creator-Sustainer- Guardian Evolver to Perfection) of the worlds'..., and how it emphasizes the humbleness, weakness and helplessness of us - His creatures in terms of: 'You alone do we worship and You alone do we implore for help.'

***Al-Saba'l Ma'sânî* السباء المثانى (the Dual Seven):** Another of the names of this Surah is *Al-Saba'l Ma'sânî* (the Dual Seven). One reason for this title is that the Surah comprises two halves, one half consists of the worshipper's homage to

[4] *<u>S</u>ahî<u>h</u> of Al-Bu<u>kh</u>ârî*

Allâh and the other half describes the bounty of Providence towards His mortal servants. It has also been said that it has been called the *masâni* (unique) because of its exceptional merits among all the Divine Books, the equal of which is not to be found in the Torah or the Gospels or in the Books of Prophets. It has also been claimed that it has been described as *masâni* because it has seven verses from Allâh, the recitation of each one being equal to their citation of one seventh of the Exalted Qur'ân'.

***Saba'*** **سبا (seven):** It has also been said that it has been named *Saba'* (seven) as it indicates seven gates of hell and each verse of this Magnificent Surah wards off the flames of one of them by the command of Allâh. Whoso therefore seeks to pass by these seven gates of hell in security, should enter this *Saba'* (seven verses haven) with eagerness and steadfast attachment to Allâh. Whatever of morals, conduct, and beliefs leads into hell, these seven verses are antidotes to the fatal poisons.

In the reported sayings of the Holy Prophet Mu<u>h</u>ammad ﷺ, several other names of this Surah are mentioned. Remember Surah *Al-Fâti<u>h</u>ah* is a treasure-house of Divine mysteries. It opens up the heart and expands the mind. Surah *Al-Fâti<u>h</u>ah* should, therefore, be read repeatedly. It is important to reflect deeply on this prayer.

**Meanings of the Word 'Surah':**

A chapter of the Qur'ân, and there are 114 of them, is called a *Surah*. This word means: (1) rank and eminence; (2) a mark or sign; (3) an elevated and beautiful edifice; and (4) something full and complete.[5] [6]

[5] *Aqrab al-Muwârid by al-<u>Kh</u>aurî al-Shartûtî*

[6] *Dictionary of the Holy Qur'ân by 'Abdul Mannân 'Omar (page 277)*

The Chapters of the Qur'ân are called *Surahs* because:
(a) One is exalted in rank by reading them and attains to eminence through them.
(b) They serve as marks for the beginning and the end of the different subjects dealt with in the Qur'an.
(c) They are each like a noble spiritual edifice.
(d) Each one of them contains a complete theme.

The name *Surah* for such a division has been used in the Qur'an itself (see 2:23 & 24:1).

It has been said in the *Sahih Muslim*: Says the Holy Prophet صلى الله عليه وسلم: "Just now a **Surah** has been revealed to me and it runs as follows ...". [7]

From this it is clear that the name **Surah** for a division of the Qur'ân has been in use from the very beginning of Islam and is not a later innovation.

## Power and Attributes of Surah *Al-Fâtihah*

**Volumes of Meaning in Few Words:** Every word of the Holy Qur'ân is affirmed by tradition, history and scientific research. Surah *Al-Fâtihah* is affirmed through a tremendous tradition and historical process. Indeed, it is recited every day, in every *raka'a* of every *Salât* (Prayer) by all Muslims around the world.

Surah *Al-Fâtihah* is a miracle. It comprises both commandments and prohibitions and grand prophecies. The Honored Qur'ân is a vast ocean. If one has to consult it in respect of some point, one should ponder well over Surah *Al- Fâtihah*. For, it is the 'Mother of the Book'. From it issue forth insights into the Noble Qur'ân.

---

[7] *Sahih by Muslim ibn Hajjâj*

All the beauties and characteristics and attributes of *Al-Fâtihah*, are demonstrably without parallel and without equal. If one were to appraise justly the excellence of those truths that are comprised in *Al-Fâtihah*, and consider the fine points and take into account its literary charm and conciseness, compressing such volumes of meaning in so few words and then glance at the splendor of its Arabic language, its fluency, its clarity, and should then contemplate its spiritual effectiveness that miraculously transforms hearts, which is beyond the reach of human capacity, would become manifest to a degree that cannot be surpassed.

## *Al-Fâtihah* comprises truth and wisdom

The truth is that Surah *Al-Fâtihah* encompasses every confirmed fact and every insight and comprises all points of truth and wisdom and answers the query of every seeker and overwhelms every assailant. It feeds every guest who desires to be entertained and provides drink for every visitor. It dispels every doubt that would lead to the brink of disaster and uproots every worry that would bring on dotage and leads back to the right path. There is no physician comparable to it for washing out the poison of sin and healing the crookedness of hearts and it leads to righteousness and certitude.

## Security in this world and the world to come

Since hell, of this life and the life to come has seven gates, Surah *Al-Fâtihah* has seven verses. Each one of its verses thus provides a means of security against one's approach to punishment in this world and the world to come.

"In view of the fact that it contains, in a condensed form, all the fundamental principles laid down in the Qur'an: the principle of God's oneness and uniqueness, of His being the originator and fosterer of the universe, the fount of all life-giving grace, the One to whom man is ultimately responsible, the only power that can really guide and help; the call to righteous action in the life of this world ("guide us the straightway"); the principle of life after death and of the organic consequences of man's actions and behavior (expressed in the term "Day of Judgment"); the principle of guidance through God's message-bearers (evident in the reference to "those upon whom God has bestowed His blessings") and, flowing from it, the principle of the continuity of all true religions (implied in the allusion to people who have lived - and erred - in the past); and, finally, the need for voluntary self-surrender to the will of the Supreme Being and, thus, for worshipping Him alone. It is for this reason that this surah has been formulated as a prayer, to be constantly repeated and reflected upon by the believer." [8]

## Goblet of truth and wisdom

Verily *Al- Fâtihah* is a holy plant that yields constantly the fruits of pure insight and fills one with drink from the goblets of truth and wisdom. When a person opens his heart to admit its light, that light enters therein and makes it aware of its mysteries, and whoso shuts this door draws, by his own act, darkness upon himself and witnesses his own ruin and joins the spiritually dead.

## Spiritual characteristics

Recitation of *Al-Fâtihah* during Prayer with full attention and full acceptance, of its teaching by the heart, brings satisfaction to the heart and mind. It dissipates darkness,

[8] *The Message of the Qur'ân: Translated and Explained by Muhammad Asad, ed.1984 (page1)*

and the Grace of Allâh (the grace of the Exalted Source of all grace) starts descending on the seeker, and the light of Divine approbation encompasses him until, step by step, he becomes the honored recipient of the Divine Mercy. Thereupon such wondrous manifestations are vouchsafed through him, by way of inspiration, acceptance of prayer, disclosure of that which is hidden; and Divine succor that the like of them is not to be witnessed in the case of another.

*Al-Fâtihah* is in truth a manifestation of Divine Light. Such marvels have been witnessed during the course of its recitation that they illustrate the dignity and eminence of the Holy Word of Allâh. By the blessings of this blissful Surah and through its regular recitation, hundreds of hidden events have been, by Divine favor, disclosed before their occurrence and every difficult situation has been cleared up in a marvelous manner by the *Aulia* (honored ones of Allâh).

Similarly, through the frequent recital of *Al-Fâtihah*, insight into spiritual marvels of many kinds have become such a phenomenal occurrence that, if even an in significant reflection of them were to be experienced by a non-Muslim divine, he would risk his very life readily and forsake all worldly cares and join Al-Islam.

## A Bright light - A Teacher - A Helper

*Al-Fâtihah* is truly at once a fortified castle, a bright light, a teacher and a helper. It secures the commandments of the Qur'ân against addition or subtraction like securing the frontiers of a realm thus preserving its integrity. It is like a reservoir with an abundant supply of water as if it were the confluence of many streams or the channel of a mighty river. The benefits of this noble Surah and its fine qualities are beyond count and defy computation and that it is not within human capacity to enumerate them, even if one were to dedicate a whole lifetime to this enterprise.

The ignorant have not appreciated it as it deserves to be appreciated. They read it, but repeated perusal does not help them to appreciate its excellences. This Surah mounts powerful assaults on those who reject it and works swiftly on sound minds. Whoso has deliberated on it analytically and has drawn close to it, pondering with a mind illumined like a bright lamp, has found it the light of the eyes and the key to secrets. This is the truth without a doubt and no conjecture. If you are in any doubt, then be up and try it yourself laying aside lethargy and indolence; and quibble not about how and when.

The recitation of Surah *Al-Fâti<u>h</u>ah* in Prayer is obligatory and it is this prayer that clearly shows that true prayer is made only in the course of the Prayer service (*<u>S</u>alât*). Allâh has taught this in this manner:

Before supplicating the Almighty one should praise and glorify Him, so that one's spirit may be uplifted with love and adoration. The *Al-Fâti<u>h</u>ah*, therefore, begins with: All worthiness of praise belongs to Allâh, the Creator and Sustainer of all Who bestows out of His pure grace, even before any action or prayer proceeds from His creatures, and then rewards righteous action in this world and in the hereafter also. He is the Master of Judgment and the Day of Requital. Every requital rests in His hands. Good and evil are in His power. One becomes a full and perfect believer in His Unity only when one accepts Allâh, the Most High, as the Supreme Master of Judgment and the Day and Time of Requital.

Beware it is a sin to regard human authorities as all-powerful in their respective spheres of control or authority.

This amounts to associating them with Allâh. As God has invested them with authority, they should be obeyed. But do not set them up as gods. Render unto man his due and render unto Allâh His due.

The next stage is of supplication: You alone do we worship and You alone do we implore for help. Guide us along the right path the path of those whom You have bestowed Your favours and blessings. That is the party of the Prophets, the Faithful Ones, the Martyrs and the Righteous. In this prayer the grace and bounty bestowed on all these groups is pleaded for. The supplication proceeds: Save us from the way of those who incurred Thy displeasure and who went astray.

## Prayer for all Humanity

In this prayer one should include:
(a) Self and all the participants in the Prayer service.
(b) All Muslims
(c) All humanity

In this manner all humanity will be included in the prayer and this is the Divine goal and purpose inculcated in this prayer.

## Effectiveness of *Al-Fâtihah*

The repetition of Surah *Al-Fâtihah* during the course of prayer is very effective. Even in a mood of mental lethargy and disinclination, this practice should be kept up with constancy. One should repeatedly affirm: You alone do we worship and You alone do we implore for help; and again: Guide us along the right path; and while in prostration one should implore: O Thou Ever Living, Self-Subsisting and All-supporting, I beseech Thy mercy.

It is most beneficial to recite Surah *Al-Fâtihah* repeatedly in the course of Prayer. During the pre-dawn voluntary prayer *(Tahajjud Prayer)* it would be helpful to supplicate over and over again: Guide us along the right path, the way of those whom Thou hast favoured; with deep concentration and humility, opening the heart for the reception of Divine Light; and to repeat: Thee alone do we worship and Thee alone do we implore for help. The repetition of these verses, by the grace of Allâh the Almighty, will lead to illumination of heart and purification of soul.

**Seeking protection against the onslaught of 'the whisperer of evil':** O seeker of insight, know that it is obligatory on one who addresses himself to the recitation of the *Al-Fâtihah* or *Al-Furqân* (the Holy Qur'ân), to seek protection against Satan as has been laid down in the Qur'ân. Satan sometimes sneaks into the preserve of Allâh, like a thief and invades the sanctuary that safeguards the innocent. Allâh, therefore, determined to shield His servants from the onslaughts of 'the subtle whisperer of Evil', while they recite *Al- Fâtihah.* And to defend them with His own weapon and fix the axe squarely on his head and rescue the unwary from their state of unawareness. He, therefore, taught His servants a formula of His own to drive off Satan who has been spurned till the Day of Judgment. The secret underlying this is that Satan is the declared enemy of people from the beginning and has planned his ruin through hidden means and by sudden assault, his most cherished wish being the destruction of the children of Adam.

Allâh planned his discomfiture through the raising of Messengers and Prophets. He did not slay Satan outright; instead He granted him respite until the dead are raised by the leave of Allâh the God of Honor and Glory. He foretold his destruction in calling him 'Satan the rejected'. That is the formula that is recited before beginning the recital of the Holy Word: 'With the name of Allâh, the Most Gracious, the Ever Merciful'.

# Verse 1

بِسْمِ اللَّـهِ الرَّحْمَٰنِ الرَّحِيمِ (١)
*With the name of Allâh,*
*the Most Gracious, the Ever Merciful.*

### Important Arabic Words Used In This Verse

**Bâ ب ; Ism اسم ; Allâh الله ;**

**Al ال Rahmân الرحمان ; Rahîm الرحيم**

***Bâ* ب*:*** According to Arab usage, the words "*Aqrau* (I recite)" or *Ashrau* (I begin)" would be taken to be understood before *Bismallâh*. *Bâ* which is sometimes translated as "In" may not convey the real essence of the meanings of *Bâ*. As "In" signifies "on account of". The expression *B-ism-Allâh* would thus mean: "I begin/recite with the help and assistance of the name of Allâh".[9]

***Ism* اسم*:*** It is derived either from *wsm* وس م or *smw* س م و.
*wsm* و س م: Distinguishing mark; name; attribute; to surpass in beauty; to bear the impress of beauty.
smw س م و : To be high and raised.

In *Bismallâh* it is used in both senses (wsm و س م and smw س م و). It refers to "Allâh" which is the personal name

---

[9] Dictionary of the Holy Qur'ân by 'Abdul Mannân 'Omar (page 40)

of the Almighty God and it refers to His attributive names like *Al-Rahmân* and *Al-Rahîm*. Moreover, Allâh is High and Raised because He is the very apex of Beauty, Love, Beneficence, Grace, and Mercy.[10]

***Allâh*** الله: *Allâh* is a proper name applied to the Being Who exists necessarily by Himself, comprising all the attributes of perfection; and Who is free from all defects and weaknesses. All Divine attributes mentioned in Al-Qur'ân are qualities of the proper name *Allâh*. It is never used as a qualifying word.

The *"al"* being inseparable from it, not derived. *al-ilâh* is a different word, and Allâh is not a contraction of *al-ilâh*.[11] [12]

**Al** ال: It is equivalent to "The" in English. In Arabic it is used to give the meaning of:
Most; All; Complete; Maximum; Whole; Comprehensive; Perfect in all degrees and grades. So Al ال would mean all of the above.[13]

***Al-Rahmân*** **الرحمان and** ***Al-Rahîm*** **الرحيم:** Both these words are derived from the same root word *Rahima* رَحِم.

Meaning: Grace; Mercy; Love; Kindness; Tenderness; Forgiveness; Pity; Goodness; Favour; Beneficence. [14] [15] [16]

***Al-Rahmân***: The Most Gracious. The One Who gives without asking and effort.

---

[10] **Dictionary of the Holy Qur'ân by 'Abdul Mannân 'Omar (page 272)*
[11] *Tâj al-Arûs and Arabic English Lexicon by E. W. Lane*
[12] **Dictionary of the Holy Qur'ân by 'Abdul Mannân 'Omar (page 28)*
[13] **Dictionary of the Holy Qur'ân by 'Abdul Mannân 'Omar (page 25)*
[14] *Mufradât fi Gharâib al-Qur'ân by Al-Raghib*
[15] *Kashshaf - Commentary by Al- Zamakhsharî*
[16] *Dictionary of the Holy Qur'ân by 'Abdul Mannân 'Omar (page 205)*

It conveys the idea of fullness and extensiveness and indicates the greatest preponderance *(-superiority in weight, power, numbers etc..)* of the quality of grace, love and mercy which comprehends the entire universe without regard to our effort and asking, even before we are born. *Al-Rahmân* is the attribute of Allâh because of His granting to every animate (-being or object having perception and choice), a shape and a constitution appropriate to his or its role.

*Al-Rahmân* bestows upon each one the faculties and powers that are best suited to the life he/it has to live, and equipped each with appropriate bodies and limbs making available to each, all that was suitable and needed for their survival.

*Al-Rahmân* created the celestial bodies and the earth thousands of years before the coming into existence of these creatures, to provide the means of sustenance and protection for them.

*Al-Rahmân* is not contingent on the work and efforts of any creature. It is pure grace, in abundance, which came into effect long before the creation of these beings and objects. *Al-Rahmân* one Who Bestows without reference to effort and without reference to prayer and without distinction between believer and disbeliever. Thus this attribute of Allâh is manifested in both the believer and the unbeliever alike.

*Al-Rahmân* is the source of Love and Mercy in the spiritual life of human beings as well. Allâh's Revelation in the form of Holy Books and Scriptures is an example in this regard.

***Rahîm* رحيم:** derived from the same root word *Rahima* رَحِمَ:

Grace; Mercy; Love; Kindness; Tenderness; Forgiveness; Pitty; Goodness; Favour; Beneficence.

*Al-Rahmân* and *Al-Rahîm* are not the repetition of one and the same attribute for the sake of emphasis but are two different attributes. *Al-Rahîm* conveys the meaning of constant repetition and manifestation of this attribute, and giving of liberal reward to those who deserve it and seek of it.

*Al-Rahîm*: Ever Merciful, Ever Loving, and Ever Dispenser of Grace and Love as a result of our deeds and supplications. *Al-Rahîm* causes good results to follow on good deeds and would not nullify and render void anyone's right and virtuous deeds and behavior.

The attribute *Al-Rahmân* circumscribes the quality of 'abounding, rich, and blissful Grace', whereas *Al-Rahîm* the 'continuous manifestation' of Grace and its effect upon us and is a liberal reward of one's deeds and supplications.[17] [18] [19]

[17] *Bahr al-Muhît by Abû Hayyân al-Andulusi*

[18] *Zâd al-Maâd by Ibn Qayyîm*

[19] . *Dictionary of the Holy Qur'ân by 'Abdul Mannân 'Omar (page 205-206)*

# Pearls of Wisdom

May Allâh grant us the knowledge of His attributes and lead us all on to the ways that please Him and guide us to the paths that have His approval.

The word ism that occurs in *Bismillah* is a derivative of *wasm* and *wasmun.* In Arabic it means the mark left by branding. In Arabic '*ittasamar rajulu*' is used when a person chooses for himself a mark of identification by means of which people distinguish him from others.

*'Simatul baeer'* and *'wisamul baeer'* are also considered derivatives of *wasmun* and mean branding a special mark on a camel to serve as its distinguishing mark. The phrase *inni tawassumtu fihilkhaira wa ma raaituzzair*, i.e. I scanned his face and found only good in it, I perceived no trace of evil in it: is also derived from the same root.

The word *wasmiyyun* is also derived from it; it means the first spring rain, for, when it falls, it leaves marks on the earth formed by the strong current of water, as springs carve out channels in their course.

Similarly they call the earth '*ardhun mausoomatun*' when the first spring rain falls on it and by its flowering pleases the heart of the cultivators.

The word '*mausimun*' (season) is also a derivative of '*wasmun*' as, for instance, '*mausimul hajj*' (the season of Pilgrimage) and '*mausimus suq*' (market season) and other '*mausims*' (seasons): for, these are occasions when people gather in large numbers for some common purpose.

The Arabs used '*wasmun*' and its derivatives generally in a eulogistic sense whether relating to worldly welfare or to spiritual well-being.

In popular parlance the *ism* (name) of a thing stands for its distinguishing mark but, in the view of the learned, it signifies its reality. It is a fact that the names given by Allâh to things signify their properties. In this blessed verse, the names Allâh, *Al-Rahmân* and *Al-Rahîm* possess that characteristic. Each one of them denotes its particular attributes and its nature.

Allâh is the name of the Being who combines in Himself all the excellences. *Al-Rahmân* and *Al-Rahîm* indicate that both these are attributes of Allâh Who combines in Himself every kind of perfection and every kind of beauty.

**Allâh - Multiplicity of Divine Attributes:** Allâh, the substantive name which combines in itself all perfect attributes, is the Supreme Name, importing vast blessings.

In the idiom of the Holy Qur'ân, Allâh is the name of Whose excellences are the culmination of beauty and beneficence, and Who does not suffer from any shortcoming. The name Allâh alone has been invested with all perfect attributes, thus the name Allâh applies only to the One Who combines in Himself all perfect attributes and no shortcomings.

Allâh is imperceptible, above the reach of reason, beyond of beyond, finer than the finest towards Whom everything turns in true worship. Allâh applies to the God Who suffers from no defect and possesses every excellence. Excellence is of two types, excellence in beauty and excellence in beneficence. Both types of excellence are comprehended in the word Allâh.

This is the first verse of Surah *Al-Fâti<u>h</u>ah* and also occurs at the beginning of the other Chapters of the Noble Qur'ân. No other verse is repeated so frequently in the Noble Qur'ân. It has become traditional in Al-Islam to recite this verse before starting on any work and enterprise, big or small, for the purpose of seeking Divine Blessings and Help.

A verity comprised in the verse: With the name of Allâh, the Most Gracious, the Ever Merciful; is that this verse is intended as introductory to the study of the Holy Qur'ân and it is recited with the object of seeking help from Allâh of Whose attributes is *Al-Ra<u>h</u>mân (The Most Gracious),* that is, the One Who provides for the seeker of truth through His sheer grace and beneficence all the means of achieving benevolence, blessing and guidance; and whose other attribute is *Al-Ra<u>h</u>îm (The Ever Merciful),* that is, the One Who does not let go waste the effort of the diligent and the enterprising and rewards it beneficently, rendering to them the healthy fruits of their labor.

*Al-Ra<u>h</u>mân* and *Al-Ra<u>h</u>im* are derived from the same root *Rahmah*. The word *Ra<u>h</u>mân* combines the idea of *Riqqah*, (tenderness) and *I<u>h</u>sân*, (goodness).[20]

*Al-Ra<u>h</u>mân* is in the measure of *Fa'lan* and *Al-Ra<u>h</u>îm* in the measure of *Fa'il.* According to the rules of the Arabic language, the larger the number of letters added to the root-word, the more extensive or more intensive does the meaning become. [21]

---

[20] *Mufradât fi <u>Gh</u>arâib al-Qur'ân by Abdul Qâsim al-<u>H</u>usain al-Râ<u>gh</u>ib*
[21] *Tafsîr Kashshâf by Zama<u>kh</u>sharî*

The measure of *Fa`lan* conveys the idea of fullness and extensiveness, while the measure of *Fa'il* denotes the idea of repetition and giving liberal reward to those who deserve it. [22]

Thus, whereas the word *Al-Rahmân* would denote "mercy comprehending the entire universe," the word *Al-Rahîm* would denote "mercy limited in its scope but repeatedly shown."

In view of the above meanings *Al- Rahmân* is One Who shows mercy gratuitously and extensively to all creation without regard to effort or work, and *Al-Rahîm* is One Who shows mercy in response to, and as a result off, the actions of a person but shows it liberally and repeatedly. The former extends not only to believers and disbelievers but also to the whole creation; the latter applies mostly to believers.

According to a saying of the Holy Prophet صلى الله عليه وسلم, the former attribute generally pertains to this life, while the latter attribute generally pertains to the life to come. [23]

Meaning that as this world is mostly the world of actions and the next world is the world where actions will be particularly rewarded, God's attribute *Al-Rahmân* provides man with material for his works in this life, and His attribute *Al-Rahîm* brings about results in the life to come.

All things that we need and on which our life depends are purely a Divine favour and are provided for us before we do anything to deserve them or even before we are born, while the blessings in store for us in the life to come will be given to us as a reward of our actions. This shows that *Al-*

---

[22] *Bahr al-Muhît by Abû Hayyan al-Andulusî*
[23] *ibid*

*Rahmân* is the Bestower of gifts which precede our birth, while *Al-Rahîm* is the Giver of blessings which follow our deeds as their reward.

**A human who is weak and ignorant may be enlightened with the help of Allâh:** Now, pay attention to the recital of some of the truths comprised in this verse. The principal purpose of the revelation of this verse is that a human who is weak and ignorant may be enlightened with 'Allâh' – the All Mighty. Allâh is the Mighty name of the Self-Existing God who comprises all perfect attributes, and is free from every weakness and defect and is alone worthy of worship, is without partner or peer, and is the source of all grace.

The Mighty Name 'Allâh' has many attributes of which two are mentioned in this verse, namely *'Al-Rahmân'* (The Most Gracious) and *'Al-Rahîm'*(The Ever Merciful). The Divine Word is revealed and its light and blessings radiate their beneficence by virtue of these two attributes:

It should be recognised that the object in prescribing the recitation of this verse before starting the recitation of the Nobel Qur'ân is that one should seek help and blessing from Allâh, the Supreme ***Rabb*** (- Creator, Sustainer, Guardian Evolver to Perfection) of all excellences, through His attributes and powers of being *Al-Rahmân* and *Al-Rahîm,* so that He, the Perfect Lord may, provide the reader all the means and hope needed for success.

It is thus the highest virtue to seek blessings and support from the Supreme, through His attributes of being *Rahmân* and *Rahîm*, before reciting the Qur'ân and indeed before embarking upon any enterprise.

Thus does a person realize the essence of Divine Unity, and his own lack of knowledge, information and insight and his error and helplessness, and then his gaze rests on the Majesty and Glory of the Source of all grace and, discovering himself an utter pauper and of no account whatever, he seeks grace from the Absolute Almighty, through His *Rahmâniyyat* and *Rahîmiyyat*.

**Objective of the Recitation of this Verse:** It should be recognised that the object in prescribing the recitation of this verse before starting the recitation of the Holy Qur'ân is that one should seek help and blessing from Allâh, the Supreme Lord of all excellences, through His attributes of *Rahmâniyyat* and *Rahîmiyyat*. So that He, the Perfect Lord may, through His *Rahmâniyyat*, provide the reader, out of pure grace and beneficence, with all the means needed by him prior to his own effort. All this emanates from the attribute of *Rahmâniyyat*.

Seeking blessing through the attribute of *Rahîmiyyat* means that the Perfect Being may crown the effort of His servant with beneficent results, safeguard him against failure and bless his enterprise after his efforts and struggle.

It is thus the highest virtue to seek blessings and support from the Supreme, through His attributes of *Rahmâniyyat* and *Rahîmiyyat*, before reciting the Divine Word and indeed before embarking upon any enterprise.

**Prayer should play a great role in the achievement of success in any endeavor:** These Divine attributes are in operation all the time, yet God has ordained from the beginning that prayer and supplication should play a great role in the achievement of success in any endeavor. Divine Grace most certainly helps resolve the difficulties of those who supplicate Him in perfect faith and utter sincerity.

Someone who is conscious of his own drawbacks and shortcomings would not embark upon any enterprise with irresponsible self-assurance. His appreciation of his standing as a creature and servant of Allâh would impel him to supplicate Allâh - the All-Powerful for help. This appreciation permeates every heart that has retained its innate simplicity and is aware of its own shortcomings.

The true human, therefore, whose soul is free from all trace of arrogance and egotism and who is fully conscious of his own weakness and ineffectiveness and finds himself in capable of achieving anything and sees naught of power and strength in his own person, before he embarks on an enterprise. He finds his feeble spirit bent on seeking heavenly aid, his gaze resting all the time on the Almighty in all His Perfection and Glory, and His *Rahmâniyyat* and *Rahîmiyyat* appear to him as the mainsprings for the effective achievement of his purpose.

Therefore, before exercising his own imperfect and ineffective energies, he spontaneously seeks Divine help through the prayer: Beseeching help 'With the name of Allâh, The Most Gracious, The Ever Merciful'. In response to his humility he is granted power from the power of Allah and strength from His strength and knowledge from His knowledge, so that He may thereby achieve success in his objective.

This does not need to be established through an involved process of reasoning. Every human soul possesses the capacity to understand this and the personal experiences of the true seekers of God furnish recurring testimony in support of it. A person's seeking help from God is not a fiction or absurdity or without firm basis in fact. It is an eternal truth that it has ever been the way of the Noble Lord Who is truly the Sustainer and Guardian Evolver of the

Universe. Allâh lends His support to those who, rating themselves as unworthy and humble, seek it in their undertakings, with the recitation of His name. By turning to Him, in genuine humility and spirit of submissiveness, they partake of His succor.

**Inaugurating every enterprise with a prayer for help from the Source of every grace:** In short, inaugurating every enterprise with a prayer for help from the Source of every grace, the *Rahmân* and the *Rahîm*, is the way of extreme reverence, submission, self-negation and utter dependence, which is the first step in the direction of realization of Divine Unity in human conduct.

By strict adherence to it a person acquires childlike humility and is washed clean of every trace of the arrogance with which the minds of the haughty worldlings are filled. Believing in his own emptiness and the reality of Divine support, he partakes of that spiritual insight, which is the special portion of the true and genuine God-seeker.

For sure, the more a person adopts this way and the more strictly he adheres to it and the more clearly he realizes that departing from it spells ruin, the clearer becomes his vision of Divine Unity. The more he is cleansed of the grime of pride and egotism and the soot of artificiality and affectation is washed off his face and it begins to radiate in the light of innocence and candor.

**Step by step leads a person to the stage of *Fanafillah*:** This, in short, is the truth that step by step leads a person to the stage of *Fanafillah* (losing oneself in Allâh) until he finds that he has nothing of his own and that whatever he receives is a bounty of God. As soon as a person starts treading along this path, he begins to perceive the perfume of Divine Unity, his mind and heart being suffused with it, provided his spiritual faculty of smell is not damaged in any way.

Briefly then, a sincere seeker must, in the pursuit of this reality, confess his own utter ineffectiveness and helplessness, and bear witness to the Omnipotence and all-embracing graciousness of God. Both these affirmations are cherished objectives of God-seekers and a necessary pre-condition of the attainment of the state of self-negation.

**The one who ask is given and the one who seek finds:** Thus only the one who asks is given and only the one who seeks finds. Those who embark upon an enterprise relying solely on their own skill or wisdom or power and do not rely on God, the Most High, have little appreciation of the Almighty Who encompasses the Universe through His Power. Their faith is like a dry twig that is no longer bound to the green and blooming tree and has become so dehydrated that it cannot draw aught of its freshness, its blossoms and its fruits. It has only an outward connection which can snap at the slightest stir in the air or at the jerk of a human hand.

Such is the faith of the sophists and theorists who do not rely on the help of the All-Sustaining Lord and, do not regard that Source of all grace whose name is Allâh, as their indispensible support. They are as alien to the true concept of Divine Unity as darkness is to light. They fail to comprehend that placing oneself under the mighty power of the All-Powerful, truly believing oneself to be powerless and helpless is the last degree of submissiveness and the utmost realization of the Unity of the Divine where the complete negation of self is achieved and one loses one's self and volition totally, affirming with a sincere faith in the overpowering might of Allah.

**Allâh's dominion over us has not been abolished:** No weight need be given to the argument that God having endowed us with appropriate faculties and capacities. It would be an act of supererogation to seek His help through prayer for success in an undertaking. It is true that God the Supreme has equipped us with certain faculties to perform certain tasks but His dominion over us has not thereby been abolished, nor has He parted from us, nor has He desired to exclude us from His support, nor has He permitted that we should be deprived of His limitless beneficence.

Besides, whatever He has bestowed on us is limited and that which is begged of Him is without limit. Also we have not the power to attain to that which is beyond our capacities.

A moment's reflection would bring home to us that we do not possess a single faculty or capacity which is complete and absolute. Take for example our physical powers. They depend on our physical health which, again, is dependent on many factors, some of the earth and others of beyond the earth, but all of them beyond our sovereign control.

This simple observation is for the benefit of an average person. But in truth the extent to which Allâh, because of His being the Prime Cause, the Cause of all causes, encompasses our exterior and our interior and our beginning and our end, above us and below us, on our right and on our left, in our hearts and our lives and our souls.

**Acceptance of prayer in its different manifestations:** An objection is raised that on occasion this seeking of Divine grace and beneficence proves of no avail and the seeker is frustrated. This reflection is generated by a misunderstanding of a great truth which is that God most certainly hears a supplication made in complete sincerity of spirit and helps the seeker in an appropriate manner, on the basis of His perfect knowledge and wisdom.

At times, it may happen that the supplication lacks sincerity and humility of spirit. The suppliant may lack faith, the words of the supplication being mere sounds, the heart of the supplicant indifferent.

It may also be that the prayer is heard, the petition is granted in the manner most appropriate and beneficial for the supplicant in God's knowledge and wisdom. A supplicant who does not appreciate the hidden beneficence of God, owing to lack of knowledge and because of his ignorance, may feel frustrated, in utter disregard of the message of the verse: [24]

وَعَسَىٰ أَنْ تَكْرَهُوا شَيْئًا وَهُوَ خَيْرٌ لَكُمْ ۖ وَعَسَىٰ أَنْ تُحِبُّوا شَيْئًا وَهُوَ شَرٌّ لَكُمْ ۗ وَاللَّهُ يَعْلَمُ وَأَنْتُمْ لَا تَعْلَمُونَ (٢١٦)

*...But it may be that a thing is hard upon you though it is (really) good for you, and it may be that you love a thing while it is bad for you. Allâh knows (all things) while you do not know. (2:216)*

It is thus clear that a grand truth is proclaimed in this verse *Bismillah ir Rahmân ir Rahîm*. It provides an excellent means for fostering of the realization of Divine Unity and the relationship subsisting between human being and his 'Creator, Sustainer and Guardian Evolver to Perfection – Allâh'.

---

[24] *The Holy Qur'ân: explained by 'Allamah Nooruddîn, rendered into English by Mrs. A. R. 'Omar; 'Abdul Mannân 'Omar*

**Why Allâh has chosen to mention only two of His attributes, *Rahmân and Rahîm*:** Here a question is raised, which needs to be set down together with its answer, so that those gifted with understanding may reflect on it.

In this verse of *Bismillah Al-Rahmân Al-Rahîm*, Allâh has chosen to mention only two of His attributes, *Rahmân and Rahîm*, out of all His numerous attributes and the verse does not mention any other Divine attribute; while His super name Allâh comprises all perfect Divine attributes, as they find mention in the Holy Scriptures, and the larger the number of Divine attributes that may be invoked the greater the blessing.

The *Bismillah Al-Rahmân Al-Rahîm* thus demands that it should be invested with the honor of comprising numerous Divine attributes. This seems to follow also from the Holy Prophet's injunction that *Bismillah Al-Rahmân Al-Rahîm* should be recited before initiating any important measure and/or enterprise. Thus this verse is the one most frequently recited by the tongues of the followers of the faith and is most often repeated in the Holy Book of Allâh.

What then is the wisdom and the philosophy underlying the omission of other Divine attributes in this blessed verse? The answer is that Allâh chose to attach in this context to His Super name Allâh the two Divine attributes that epitomize fully all His other great and innumerable attributes , and these two are '*Rahmân' and 'Rahîm'*.

Reason also points in the same direction. *Allâh* manifests Himself in the universe at times as the Lover (through His attribute of *Rahmân – Grace and Benevolence*), and at times as the Beloved (through His attribute of *Rahîm* – Mercy and Compassion), and these two attributes shed the light of the sun of Providence upon the earth of obedience.

*Allâh* in turn becomes the Beloved with the worshipper becoming the Seeker (lover) of this sought-after (beloved) and at times the worshipper becomes the object of love (beloved) and God his Lover, choosing him as His objective.

There is not the least doubt that human nature is endowed with love, friendliness and yearning. Human yearns for a Beloved who should draw him towards Himself through manifestations of beauty and bounty. And that he should have a loving and comforting Friend Who should stand by him in times of fear and distress, secure him against the failure of his effort and fulfill his hopes.

Allâh, therefore, determined upon granting a human being in full measure that which his nature demanded and to perfect His favour unto him through His vast bounty. He, therefore, chose to manifest Himself to humans through His attributes of *Rahmân* (Grace and Beneficence) and *Rahîm* (Mercy and Compassion).

There is no doubt that these two attributes are a link between Divine Providence and human submission and by means of these two the circle of human insight into the Divine and human journey towards Him becomes complete. All other Divine attributes are comprehended in the refulgent light of these two attributes and are but drops in the vastness of the oceans of Allah's attributes.

Again, just as Allâh the Supreme determined for Himself that He should be for human being both the Beloved and the Lover so He determined in respect of His most obedient servants that they too should be, for their fellow-human beings, in their characters and dispositions, reflections of His attributes, making these two attributes their coverings and garments, and there should be left no deficiency in the spiritual evolution of humanity.

He thus raised Prophets and Messengers as mirrors, some reflecting His attribute *Rahmân* (Grace and Beneficence) and others portraying His attribute *Rahîm* (Mercy and Compassion) so that they should be both seekers and sought, loving and loved, living in mutual accord and affection through His Vast Grace, granting to some of them a large share of the attribute of being loved and to others a large share of the attribute of loving.

## Significance of Muhammad محمد and Ahmad احمد:

Allâh the Exalted said: [25]

وَمَا أَرْسَلْنَاكَ إِلَّا رَحْمَةً لِلْعَالَمِينَ (١٠٧)

*"And We did not send you (O Muhammad) but as a blessing and mercy for all beings". (21:107).*

It is well known that the two attributes *'Rahmân'* and *'Rahîm'* are the highest among all the attributes of Allâh. In fact, these two are the quintessence and the core of the reality of all His attributive names. Indeed they are yardsticks for the spiritual evolution of a seeker who strives after perfection through becoming a manifestation of Divine attributes.

Allâh named our Prophet *'Muhammad'* and *'Ahmad'*, as He named Himself *'Al-Rahmân'* and *'Al-Rahîm'*, in this verse. This juxtaposition indicates that no one combines these two concepts to perfection in his person by way of reflection except our Chief, the choicest of creation, the Seal of the Prophets, Muhammad ﷺ.

[25] *The Holy Qur'ân: explained by 'Allamah Nooruddîn, rendered into English by Mrs. A. R. 'Omar; 'Abdul Mannân 'Omar*

No one has been granted a complete measure of these two attributes of Allâh except our Holy Prophet صلى الله عليه وسلم, the culmination of the Prophetic dispensation. He has been given two names by the grace of the Lord of the heavens and the earth parallel to these two attributes, the first being *Muhammad* and the second *Ahmad.*

The name *Muhammad* thus donned the cloak of the attribute *Rahmân*, manifesting himself in the raiment of glory and beloved ness and has been praised exceedingly for his benefaction and beneficence. The name *Ahmad* appeared in the robe of the attribute *Rahîm* and the role of lover and beauty by Allâh's mercy. Thus the two names of our Holy Prophet (on whom be the peace and blessings of Allâh) are reflections of the two attributes of our Bounteous Lord, reflected in two mirrors facing one another.

Allâh named him Muhammad to indicate his quality of a 'loved one'; and He named him Ahmad to indicate his quality of 'one loving and adoring'.

The name *Muhammad* was given because people do not praise highly and frequently any one unless such a one becomes the object of their love. The name *Ahmad* was given because no one praises highly and frequently unless he loves devotedly.

There is no question, therefore, that the name *Muhammad* carries with it the sense of being loved with unfailing consistency, and similarly, the name *Ahmad* carries with it, by the grace of Allâh, the sense of loving with ardor and zeal.

There is not the least doubt that our Prophet was named *Muhammad*, because Allâh had determined to make him beloved in His own sight and in the eyes of the righteous; and by the same token, He named him *Ahmad*, since He had determined that he should be a lover of His and also a lover of the faithful believers. He is, therefore, *Muhammad* in one aspect and *Ahmad* in the other.

# Verse 2

الْحَمْدُ لِلَّـهِ رَبِّ الْعَالَمِينَ (٢)

*"All type of perfect and true praise belongs to Allâh alone, the Lord of the worlds.*

## Important Arabic Words Used In This Verse

*Al* ال; *Hamd* حمد; *Allâh* الله; *Rabb* رب; *'Alamîn* عالمين

**Al** ال: It is equivalent to the definite article "The" in English. In Arabic it is used to give the meaning of: Most; All; Complete; Maximum; Whole; Comprehensive; Perfect in all degrees and grades. So Al ال would mean all of the above. In Arabic 'Al' is also used to denote comprehensiveness, that is to say all aspects or categories of a subject, or to denote perfection, which is also an aspect of comprehensiveness, inasmuch as it includes all degrees and grades. It is also used to indicate something which has already been mentioned, or a concept of which is present in the mind.[26]

***Hamd*** حمد: Glory and Praise which is always true. This word not only includes the idea of glorification, praise, and thankfulness but also has reference to the intrinsic qualities and attributes (-by its very nature) of the object of praise and glory (-Allâh). Thus, the ultimate and true reality of *Hamd* is the exclusive due

[26] *Dictionary of the Holy Qur'ân by 'Abdul Mannân 'Omar (page 25)*

only of Allâh, Who is the source of all perfect attributes, and Who exercises those attributes deliberately and not in ignorance and under compulsion. *Hamd* is used in response to such acts (of Allâh) as are praiseworthy, admirable, laudable, and according to HIS Own choice. It is a glorification and true praise which is offered in appreciation of commendable action of One Worthy of Praise. *Hamd* also implies the humility, lowliness, and submissiveness in the person who offers it. [27] [28] [29]

There are four words in Arabic which are used, in varying significance, in the sense of praise and thankfulness:

***Madah*** مدح: gives a somewhat similar meaning as *Hamd* but whereas *Madah* may be false, *Hamd* is always true. The Holy Prophet ﷺ said, 'Throw dust in the faces of those who praise falsely'.

***Thanâ*** ثنا: The root meaning of the word being REPETITION. It indicates an idea of publicity. The emphasis in *thanâ* ثنا is more on publicity than on personal experience.
***Shukr*** شكر: (Thanks). It has limited orientation and scope. When used about man, expresses recognition of, and thankfulness for, benefits received. Whereas *Hamd* is more comprehensive in scope, and has reference to the intrinsic qualities of the object of praise. [30]

The expression "All true and perfect praise belongs to Allah alone" is much wider and deeper in significance than "I praise Allah," because a person can praise God only according to his knowledge, but the clause "all perfect and

[27] *Mufradât fi Gharâib al-Qur'ân by Al-Raghib*
[28] *The Arabic English Lexicon, E. W. Lane*
[29] *Dictionary of the Holy Qur'ân by 'Abdul Mannân 'Omar (page 135)*
[30] *ibid*

true praise belongs to Allah alone" comprises not only the praise which a person knows, but also the praise which he does not know. God is worthy of praise at all times, independently of a person's imperfect knowledge or realization.

**Muhammad and Ahmad are derivatives of *Hamd*:** The word *al-Hamd* is an infinitive and as such can be interpreted both as a subject and as an object. Interpreted as a subject, *al-Hamdu Lillahi* means, God alone has the right to bestow true praise. Interpreted as an object; it signifies that all true praise and every kind of praise in its perfection is due to God alone.

Muhammad and Ahmad are derivatives of *Hamd*. These are the two manifestations of *Hamd* (glorification):
Ahmad: One who constantly glorify Allâh
Muhammad: The Praised one (by Allâh and Muslims).

***Rabb*** رب: Is an attribute of Allâh. Means:

**Meanings:** Master; Ruler; Chief; Determiner; Creator; Originator; Regularizor; Provider; Nourisher; Maintainer; Sustainer; Developer; Evolver; Perfecter; Rewarder.

*Rabb* also means the originator of things and who combines to create new forms. *Rabb* also means the lawgiver who frames laws under which He propounds the shape which things must assume and the ratio and proportion in which various ingredients must combine with each other. *Rabb* is the arranger and evolver of the different stages through which creation have to pass on their way to final development, completion and the state of the highest perfection. *Rabb* also points to The Law of Evolution in physical and spiritual worlds. [31] [32] [33]

[31] *Mufradât fi Gharâib al-Qur'ân by Al-Raghib*

***'Alâmîn* عالمين**: Is the plural of *'alim*, which is derived from the root word *'Alama* علم.

**Meanings:** Mark; Sign; Distinguish; Knowledge; Information. [34]

It also means all creation including all categories of existence, in physical and spiritual sense. It includes animate (having perception and choice) and inanimate creation. It includes angels, human being, animal world, plant kingdom, aquatic life, heavenly bodies, the sun, the moon, the stars, etc. There are many worlds, as for example, Spiritual world, Physical world, world of thoughts and wisdom, the world of information and knowledge.

Hence, this word has come to be applied to 'all creation' and 'signs' by means of which one is able to know the Creator. The Holy Qur'ân applies this word to all creation of the heavens and the earth and of all that lies between the two. Sometimes this word is used in a restricted sense. [35] [36]

---

[32] *Arabic English Lexicon by E. W. Lane*

[33] *Dictionary of the Holy Qur'ân by 'Abdul Mannân 'Omar (page 197)*

[34] *. Dictionary of the Holy Qur'ân by 'Abdul Mannân 'Omar (page 383)*

[35] *ibid*

[36] *Dictionary of Tâj al-'Arûs by Murtdzâ Husaînî*

# Pearls of Wisdom

In the language of the Holy Qur'ân, Allâh is that Perfect God Who is rightfully adored, combining in Himself all perfect attributes, and free from every defect, the One without associate and the Source of all beneficence. Allâh in the Noble Qur'ân, made His name 'Allâh' comprehensive of all His other names and attributes and has not accorded that status to any other name.

Allâh commenced His Book with *Hamd* (true praise and glorification) and not with *shukr* (gratitude) or *madh* (praise) for *Hamd* comprises the sense of the other two and is their substitute par Excellence.

According to many scholars *shukr* (gratitude) differs from *hamd* in the sense that its application is restricted to beneficent qualities and *madh* differs from *hamd* in the sense that it applies to involuntary beneficence also. This is fully appreciated by rhetoricians and scholars.

Indeed all perfect praise and glory is due to the Rightfully Worshipped Being, Who combines in Himself **the aggregate of all Perfect excellences** and whose name is Allâh.

The meaning of *Al-hamdu lillahe* then is that all type of perfect and true Praise and Glory, whether relating to external aspects or internal realities, whether relating to inherent excellences or as manifested in natural phenomena, is due exclusively to Allâh. No other shares in it.

Whatever true praise or perfect excellence the wisdom of the wise can imagine or the minds of thinkers can contemplate belong to Allâh the Supreme. There is no excellence of which sane reason can contemplate the possibility but which Allâh lacks.

In other words, reason is not able to conceive of any excellence which is not comprehended among Divine attributes. He has all the excellences. He is Perfect in His Being, in His attributes and qualities, in every respect and is totally free from every defect and shortcoming.

Moreover, it is a refutation of the worshippers of creations and idols. They praise their false deities and ascribe to them the attributes of Allâh; whereas *Al-Hamd* - true praise and glory belongs to Allâh **alone**.

**The true reality of *Hamd* is the due only of the God Who is the source of all grace and light:** *Hamd* is a true and honest praise which is offered in appreciation of commendable action of one worthy of praise: it also means lauding one who has done a favor of his own volition and according to his own choice. The true reality of *Hamd* is the due only of the God Who is the source of all grace and light. And exercises beneficence deliberately and not in ignorance or under compulsion.

All this is found only in Allâh, the All-Knowing, the All-Seeing. Indeed He is the true Benefactor and from Him proceed all benefits from beginning to end, and for Him is all glorification, in this world and in the hereafter and all praise that is bestowed on others reverts to Him.

**Allâh receives perfect praise and also bestows it:** The word *Hamd*, used in this verse by Allâh the Lord of Glory, is the stem/root and is used both in the active and the passive sense, that is, it is used both for the subject and the object and it signifies that Allâh receives perfect praise and also bestows it on others of His choosing.

This interpretation derives support from the fact that Allâh has followed up the word *Hamd* with the mention of attributes that entail this meaning in the view of the discerning.

In the word *Hamd,* Allâh has signified the qualities that subsist in His Eternal Light. In defining *Hamd*, He has treated it as a veiled reality that uncovers its face on the recitation of the attributes *Rahmân* and *Rahîm*; for *Rahmân* signifies that *Hamd* is used in the active sense and *Rahîm* signifies that it is used in the passive sense, as is not hidden from those who possess knowledge.

**Perfect praise and glory is the exclusive prerogative of Allâh - the Lord of Majesty:** *Hamd* is praise and glorification which is offered to honor a mighty and noble for His acts of beneficence. Perfect praise and glory is the exclusive prerogative of the Lord of Majesty. The ultimate goal of every kind of glorification,

be it in a small or a large measure, is our Lord Who guides the misguided and exalts the lowly and is the object of praise of all who are praiseworthy.

Since the idolaters used to praise their idols without any justification, preferring the use of the word, *Hamd* for them, believing them to be sources of favours and bounties, and their mourning females vied with one another in boastful enumeration of the valorous deeds of their dead in battlefields and at banquets and praised them in the manner in which Allâh, the Bestower, the Guardian, the Guarantor should be praised. Hence this verse is their rebuttal, and, of all who associate partners with Allâh, and furnishes an admonition for those who use their judgment.

In these words Allâh reproaches all those who associate partners with Allâh, as if He was saying: Why do you glorify your associate-gods and why do you magnify your ancestors? Are they your lords who sustain you? Or are they the compassionate ones who treat you mercifully, ward off calamities and avert evil and affliction, safeguard the good that has been your lot, or wash off the dirt of your sufferings and cure you of your diseases? Or are they the lords of the Day of Judgment?

Nay, Allâh alone sustains and shows Mercy by granting happiness in full measure and by the grant of means of guidance and by answering prayers and by deliverance from enemies and He shall certainly reward those who work righteousness.

**Allâh possess all perfect excellences that inspire the heart spontaneously with admiration:** *Alhamdu lillahe* which means that all perfect and true praise and all glorifications belongs to Allâh. This is inspired by the purpose that the worship of Allâh, the Supreme, must be characterized by the fervor of the soul and a strong inclination, animated by love and ardor, which cannot ravel up, unless it is established that the object of worship is the Deity, possessing all perfect excellences that inspire the heart spontaneously with admiration.

It is obvious that comprehensive praise is inspired by two qualities, the perfection of beauty and the perfection of beneficence. If a being combines both these excellences, the heart melts and yearns for him with fervent devotion. The Holy Qur'ân aims at impressing these two excellences of the Supreme Being upon the seekers after Truth, so that humanity may be drawn to that peerless and unique God, and worship Him with fervent devotion and yearning. That is why in the very opening chapter, this charming description has been set forth to demonstrate the wonderful excellences of the Divine to whom the Holy Qur'ân invites humanity.

Thus this verse begins with *Al<u>h</u>amdu lillahe*, which means that all true and perfect praise belongs to the Divine Being called Allâh. In the terminology of the Holy Qur'ân, Allâh is the Being all of Whose excellences are the culmination of beauty and beneficence, and Who suffers not from any shortcoming or defect. Allâh alone comprises all attributes according to the Holy Qur'ân, and thus the name Allâh is justified for that Being alone in Whom all excellent attributes culminate. As, therefore, every kind of excellence centers in Him, the perfection of His beauty is established.

It is because of this perfect beauty that Allâh, the Supreme, has been called Light in the Holy Qur'ân:[37]

اللَّـهُ نُورُ السَّمَاوَاتِ وَالْأَرْضِ ۚ مَثَلُ نُورِهِ كَمِشْكَاةٍ فِيهَا مِصْبَاحٌ ۖ الْمِصْبَاحُ فِي زُجَاجَةٍ ۖ الزُّجَاجَةُ كَأَنَّهَا كَوْكَبٌ دُرِّيٌّ يُوقَدُ مِنْ شَجَرَةٍ مُبَارَكَةٍ زَيْتُونَةٍ لَا شَرْقِيَّةٍ وَلَا غَرْبِيَّةٍ يَكَادُ زَيْتُهَا يُضِيءُ وَلَوْ لَمْ تَمْسَسْهُ نَارٌ ۚ نُورٌ عَلَىٰ نُورٍ ۗ يَهْدِي اللَّـهُ لِنُورِهِ مَنْ يَشَاءُ ۚ وَيَضْرِبُ اللَّـهُ الْأَمْثَالَ لِلنَّاسِ ۗ وَاللَّـهُ بِكُلِّ شَيْءٍ عَلِيمٌ (٣٥)

*Allâh is the Extensive Light of the heavens and the earth. His light can be compared to a (lustrous) pillar on which a lamp is put. The lamp is inside a crystal globe. The globe of*

[37] *The Holy Qur'ân: explained by 'Allamah Nooruddîn, rendered into English by Mrs. A. R. 'Omar; 'Abdul Mannân 'Omar*

*glass is as if it were a glittering star. It (- the lamp) is lit by (the oil of) a blessed olive tree which belongs neither to the east nor to the west (rather welds the whole world in its fold). Its oil is likely to glow forth of itself even if no fire touch it. This (lamp) is a combination of many lights over and over. Allâh guides towards His light whoever desires (to be enlightened). And Allâh sets forth excellent parables for the people, and Allâh alone has full knowledge of everything. (24:35).*

**Cognition of Allâh through His Attributes and Excellences:** There is yet another direction in the word *Hamd*. Allâh, the Exalted and Lord of blessings, says: O My servants, know Me through My attributes and recognize Me through My excellences. I certainly do not suffer from any defect or shortcoming. Nay, My Praiseworthiness far exceeds the highest limits of praise rendered by those who praise Me. You will not find in the heavens or in the earth any praise worthy feature that is not to be found in My countenance.

If you tried to count My excellences you would not be able to number them, even if you exerted yourselves hard and took pains like the dedicated. Search well then if you can find a praiseworthy merit that you do not find in Me or can discover an excellence that is beyond Me and My presence. If you feel that way then you have no knowledge of Me and are bereft of vision. I am known through My glories and excellences and the heavy clouds saturated with My blessings indicate the plenitude of My bounties.

Those who believe in Me, are indeed the people who are treading the paths that lead to true recognition of Me. They have grasped the Truth and they will be successful. Thus seek earnestly for the attributes of Allâh, the Glorious, and reflect over them like deep thinkers.

Seek diligently and ponder every aspect of perfection searching for it in every overt and covert manifestation of this universe as a greedy person occupies himself incessantly with the pursuit of the object of his desires. When you arrive at the comprehension of the fullness of His perfection and begin to perceive His fragrance, it is then that you have found Him. This is a mystery that is unveiled only to those who are earnest seekers of guidance.

We should reflect particularly over those attributes of His which have been manifested in His works, that is to say, His might, His power, His dominance and His bounteousness. Then be mindful of it and neglect it not. Be sure that all Providence belongs to Allâh and all *Rahmâniyyat* belongs to Allâh and all *Rahîmiyyat* belongs to Allâh and all sovereignty belongs to Allâh on the Day of Judgment. Withhold not, therefore, your obedience from your Sustainer and be of those who submit themselves wholly to the One Lord.

This verse also connotes that Allâh, the Supreme, is far above every suspicion of weakness or shortcoming, such as the assumption of a new attribute on the decline of another attribute, or a change in His status or dignity, or developing a defect, or any kind of renewal or rehabilitation. On the contrary, to Him belongs all worthiness of praise in the beginning and in the end, manifestly and covertly, for ever and ever more. Whoever says aught contrary to this repudiates the Truth.

**This verse refutes the idol-worshippers:** This verse refutes the non-believers and the idol-worshippers, for they do not render to Allâh His just due and do not look forward to the spreading of His light. Instead, they seek to stretch over Him coverings of darkness, to abandon Him in the paths of tribulation, to divest Him of perfect excellence and to associate with Him a number of His creatures. This is an error that has ruined them and this is the blind tradition that has proved a disaster for them. Reliance on the words of fabricators has destroyed them and they fancy they are following the truth.

They pay no attention to the blunders of their predecessors, the ignorance of their leaders and their straying far away from the basic teachings of their Prophets and Messengers of God. And they wander uphill and down dale in distraction.

One wonders at their lack of understanding and sense! They do not realize that Allâh is Perfect in every respect, admitting of no defect, shortcoming, decrepitude, change or replacement. They attribute to Him a great many of these, ascribing to Him every failure, loss, defect and weakness.

In the phrase *Alhamdu lillahe*, Muslims have been taught that when they are asked: Who is your Lord?, each one of them must say: My Lord is the One to Whom all perfect and true praise is due and there is no excellence or power but is found in Him in perfection. Be not, therefore, of those who are apt to forget.

**All praiseworthy qualities that are observed in the world as existing in created objects are, in fact, attributable to Allâh:** Any excellence that subsists in an object is in reality an emanation from 'the Fashioner' That is to say, the sun does not illumine the world, in truth Allâh illumines it. Nor does the moon dispel the darkness of night, in truth Allâh dispels it. Nor do the clouds pour down water, in truth Allâh sends it down.

Similarly, what our eyes see is through the Divine gift of sight; and what our ears hear is through the Divine gift of the faculty of hearing, and what wisdom discovers is indeed through Him and whatever excellent qualities heavenly and earthly elements disclose and all the beauty and freshness that are manifested, are in reality attributable to the Creator who has clothed all these objects with perfection through His own excellence.

He did not stop at that, but invested everything with an accompanying mercy which sustains and supports it. Further, He fosters and evolves everything to its highest point of perfection, thus demonstrating its full value and utility. Obviously, then, He is the true Benefactor who comprehends all excellences.

It is to this that this verse draws attention, in its opening verses: All perfect and true praise belongs to Allâh alone, the Creator-Sustainer and Guardian Evolver of all the worlds, Most Gracious, Ever Merciful, Master of the day of Requital.

How comprehensive is then the concept of the Unity of Allâh comprehended in *Alhamdu lillahe*. It affirms that everything in the universe is in subjection to Allâh, and is not in itself a source of profit or weal, and definitely and clearly impresses on the mind that all profit and weal truly emanate from Allâh, the Supreme Lord, for, all praise belongs to Him alone.

### Muhammad and Ahmad are derivatives of *Hamd:*

The Noble Qur'ân begins with *Alhamdu lillahe* (All perfect and true praise and glory belongs to Allâh alone), to draw attention to the name of the Holy Prophet – **Muhammad** and **Ahmad** - blessing and peace of Allâh be on him.

**Muhammad** and **Ahmad** are derivatives of *Hamd* and these were two names of the Holy Prophet (pbuh). In other words, these were two manifestations of *Hamd* (glorification).

*Rabb Al-'Âlamîn* رَبِّ الْعَالَمِينَ: **Creator, Sustainer and Guardian Evolver to Perfection of all the worlds:** According to *Lisanal Arab* and *Tajul Arus*, the two most authentic lexicons, the Arabic word *RABB* has at least **seven connotations**, namely: *Mâlik* (Supreme Master), *Sayyad* (Chief), *Mudabbir* (Determiner) *Murabbi* (Provider), *Qayûm* (Sustainer), *Mun'im* (Rewarder), *Mutammim* (Perfecter). Of these seven three are connotative of Divine greatness. One of these is *Mâlik*. In Arabic *Mâlik* is one whose hold on that which he owns is complete and who can use it in any way he pleases and who has sole title to it, with no one having any share in it. In the fullest sense of its meaning it is NOT applicable to any one besides Allâh, the Most High.

"The Arabic word *Rabb*, usually translated Lord, has also the meaning of cherishing, sustaining, bringing to maturity. Allah cares for all the worlds He has created. There are many worlds - astronomical and physical worlds, worlds of thought, spiritual world, and so on. In every one of them, Allah is all-in-all."[38]

*'Âlamîn (All the worlds – known or unknown to humans):*
In His word 'Âlamîn, Allâh points out that He is the Creator of everything and from Him has emanated everything that is in all the heavens and in all the earths.

Allâh possesses many varieties of beneficence. Of these few are basic. According to their natural order, the first is the ***Rabb Al 'Âlamîn*** – Creator, Sustainer and Guardian Evolver to Perfection of all the worlds, as stated in this verse.

---

[38] *The Meaning of the Holy Qur'ân by 'Abdullah Yûsuf 'Alî, Tenth Edition (page 14)*

The *Rabbûbiyat* (Divine Providence*)* – i.e. creating, sustaining and evolving in stages to the desired perfection - is operative and pervasive throughout *Al 'Âlamîn* - i.e. All Universe, in the heavens, in the earth, in bodies, in souls, in the realm of knowledge, substance and in the realm of essence and in animals, vegetables and minerals and all other realms. All these worlds are sustained by His Providence.

A human being receives sustenance from the spring of Divine Providence, from the early embryonic, even pre-embryonic state, to the time of death, and beyond in the stage of life in the hereafter. The Providence of Allâh, because of its extending over all spirits and bodies and beasts and vegetables and minerals and the rest. has been called the most universal benevolence. For, every object that is extant is the beneficiary of this Divine attribute and every entity owes its very existence to *Rabb Al 'Âlamîn.*

Divine Providence *(RABB)* is thus the creator of every existing thing and sustainer of every extant object, yet it is a human that benefits most by it, for the entire creation of Allâh is of service to humanity. A human has, therefore, been reminded that his Allâh is the *Rabb Al 'Âlamîn* (Lord and Providence of the Universe), so that the horizon of his hopes may be extended and he may believe that Allâh, the Supreme, has immense beneficial powers and that He can bring into being for his benefit.

**The word *Al-'Âlamîn* encompasses all – *Guided* and Misguided:** The word *Al-'Âlamîn* encompasses all that is found in the world, of the groups of the guided as well as the parties of the misguided and the lost. At times, the *'Âlam* (realm) of misguidance and disbelief and transgression and excess flourishes until the earth becomes full of injustice and tyranny and people abandon the ways of Allâh, the Lord of Majesty.

They appreciate not the true nature of the relationship subsisting between the Creator and His creatures and do not render that which is due to Him as Provider and Sustainer. The world becomes dark like the blackest night and faith is pulverized under this affliction.

Then Allâh initiates another *'Âlam* (realm) and the earth is replaced with another earth and a fresh decree descends from heaven and people are granted perceiving hearts and eloquent tongues to render thanks to Allâh for His bounties.

**Spiritual people are needed most when many people turn into beasts and animals:** Spiritual people are needed most when through degradation of their condition many people turn into beasts and animals. It is at this moment that Divine compassion and His eternal favor urge that a person be raised in heavens, should dispel darkness, and demolish that which Satan has built and raised up.

Then an Imâm (spiritual leader) descends from the *Al-Rahmân* (the Gracious God) to fight the armies of Satan and these two forces join battle – but only those perceive them who are gifted with insight -until falsehood is fettered and its mirage-like reasoning is obliterated.

**The most honored are the group of Prophets and Apostles and the righteous, the true devotees of Allâh:** The most honored of all the worlds and the most marvelous of the whole of creation are the group of Prophets and Apostles and the righteous, the true servants of Allâh, for they excel all the rest, in propagating righteousness. They remove injustices, reforming conduct and inculcating peace and truthfulness.

They turn to Allâh, persisting in obedience to Allâh with full strength, mounting assault on the progeny of Satan with mustered troops and organized bodies, withdrawing from the world for the sake of the Beloved creator. They surely are a people whose eyes are overtaken by sleep while they are still absorbed in their love for Allâh and in prayer for their people.

The most honored, the most God-conscious and the most knowledgeable of them all, is our beloved Prophet Muhammad, salutations and peace be on him both in this world and in the high heavens. Yes, of the 'Âlamîn there was an *'Âlam* when the Seal of the Prophets – Muhammad صلى الله عليه وسلم was raised.

**Allâh's praise is celebrated by His worshipers - who are ever occupied with His remembrance:** Allâh, the Holiest, is *Rab al-'Âlamîn.* He is the Creator of everything and is praised highly in the heavens and in the earth and that His praise is celebrated constantly by His servants and devotees who are ever occupied with His remembrance.

When one of His servants discards his own desires, is emptied of his passions, is wholly centered in Allâh, His ways and His worship, and knows His Lord Who nurtured him by His favor, he glorifies Him all the time loving Him with all his heart, even with all the particles of his body. Such a one also becomes an *'Âlam* (a world) one of the *'Âlamîn* (the worlds).

*'Âlamîn* thus covers, with the exception of the Creator Himself, every existing thing, whether in the realm of spirits or in the realm of bodies, whether of earthly creation or like the sun, the moon or other celestial objects, all of them being *'Âlamîn* abiding under the providence of Allâh.

There is not a thing but celebrates His praise and glorifies Him all the time.

**Allâh is the *Rabb* of the World of Element and Command:** The expression employed here is not *<u>K</u>haliq-al-'Âlamîn* (Creator of the worlds); but *Rabb-al-'Âlamîn* (the Lord Creator-Sustainer and Guardian Evolver of all the worlds).

Since *<u>Kh</u>alq* connotes fashioning and putting together, Divine wisdom employed here the expression. *Rabb-al-'Âlamîn* which is more comprehensive and is also designed to indicate that He is the Rabb of the world of elements and command also, for elements proceed from command and compounds are fashioned.

**Allâh's *Grace and Providence not confined to one* people:** *Al-<u>H</u>amdulillahe-Rabbil-'Âlamîn* which means that all holy and perfect attributes are exclusively possessed by Allâh Who is the Lord-Sustainer and Guardian Evolver of the Universe. The word *'Âlamîn* (worlds) covers all nations, all ages and all lands. As such Allâh is the most praise worthy and Highly Glorified.

This verse constitutes a refutation of those who seek to confine the Providence and Grace of God to their own people and race. In other words believing that other communities and races were not created by God, or that after creating them God had rejected them or had forgotten them.

It is thus established that the true and perfect God - Allah whom every person must accept and believe in is *Rabbil-'Âlamîn* - the Lord of Universal Providence. His Providence is not confined to any particular people, race, religion, time or nationality. He is the Lord, of all peoples, all ages, all places and the source of all grace' and every physical and spiritual capacity proceeds from Him and everything that exists is sustained by Him. He is the support of every creature. His Grace comprehends all peoples, all lands and all epochs.

Thus it is so that no people may have cause to complain that Allâh was gracious towards some people and not towards others, or that a particular people was given a Book so that it may be guided thereby and another was not, or that He manifested Himself through His words and revelation and signs in a certain age but remained hidden in another age. By extending His Providence universally He disposed of all such objections and exercised such universal benevolence that no people or age was denied the beneficence of His material and spiritual grace.

The Holy Qur'ân says: [39]

إِنَّا أَرْسَلْنَاكَ بِالْحَقِّ بَشِيرًا وَنَذِيرًا ۚ وَإِنْ مِنْ أُمَّةٍ إِلَّا خَلَا فِيهَا نَذِيرٌ (٢٤)

*Verily, We have sent you with the lasting truth (as) a Bearer of glad-tidings and (as) a Warner (to them), for there has been no people but have (been warned by) a Warner (from God). (35.24).*

**All powers working in the Universe do not operate on their own, Divine power operates through them:** It is beyond doubt that all the qualities and capacities with which the celestial bodies and earthly elements are temporarily invested are but a reflection of the spiritual power and attributes eternally possessed by Allâh, the Supreme.

---

[39] *The Holy Qur'ân: explained by 'Allamah Nooruddîn, rendered into English by Mrs. A. R. 'Omar; 'Abdul Mannân 'Omar*

Allâh has made it plain to us that the sun and other bodies are nothing in themselves - it is His dominating Power that operates in them, as it were, from behind a screen. He makes the moon shed light in dark nights serving as a reflector for His light as He illumines dark hearts.

He manifests a glorious light by His power through the instrumentality of the sun and makes manifest His multifarious designs in various ways. It is His power that descends from the sky in the form of rain and revives and refreshes the dry earth and provides drink for the thirsty. It is His Power that invests fire with the quality of combustion and invests the air with the quality to refresh life, make flowers blossom forth, lift clouds and convey sound.

Then, are all these things God? Indeed not; they, are only created things. But Divine power manifests itself through them. As the power of the hand manifests itself through the pen, we say the pen writes but, in fact, it is the hand and not the pen that does the writing. A piece of iron which is left in the fire for a time assumes the qualities of fire and we say that it burns and emits light; but these are not its own properties, they are the properties of fire.

By the same token it is true that all the heavenly bodies and earthly elements, indeed every particle in the lower and upper spheres that is visible and perceptible, all of them are, by virtue of the various properties that are found in them, so many names and attributes of God. It is the power of God that manifests itself through them. These are all His words which His power made manifest in different forms.

One not aware might ask, how did the words of God acquire material shape? Did God suffer diminution by sending them forth? A magnifying glass, by reflecting the rays of the sun, may ignite a fire, but that causes no diminution in the power of the sun. Fruits are fostered and ripen under moonbeams but that does not wear down the moon. This is the truth that furnishes insight into Divine working and is at the center of all spiritual phenomena that the universe has come into existence through the words of Allâh.

**The universe does not operate on its own, but that Divine power operates through it:** The verse *Al-Hamdu lillahe Rabbil-'Âlamîn* of this *Surah Al-Fâtihah* indicates that all the forces in operation in the heavens and the earth in various shapes and forms to ensure the proper running of the universe do not operate on their own, but that Divine power operates through them. The same idea is expressed in another verse that the world is like a palace with floors paved with transparent glass, under which runs a strong current of water. An unaware person ignores the glass and is afraid to step in lest he should tumble into the swift current.

It is also stated in the Holy Qur'ân: [40]

وَلَقَدْ كَرَّمْنَا بَنِي آدَمَ وَحَمَلْنَاهُمْ فِي الْبَرِّ وَالْبَحْرِ وَرَزَقْنَاهُمْ مِنَ الطَّيِّبَاتِ
وَفَضَّلْنَاهُمْ عَلَىٰ كَثِيرٍ مِمَّنْ خَلَقْنَا تَفْضِيلًا (٧٠)

*And most surely We have made the Children of Adam greatly honoured and have carried them over land and sea, and We have provided them with good and pure things and have distinctly exalted them far above most of Our creation. (17:70)*

[40] *The Holy Qur'ân: explained by 'Allamah Nooruddîn, rendered into English by Mrs. A. R. 'Omar; 'Abdul Mannân 'Omar*

The expression *Rabb al-'Âlamîn* is most comprehensive. If it were established that any of the heavenly bodies are inhabited their habitations and their dwellers would be covered by this expression.

# Verse 3

الرَّحْمَٰنِ الرَّحِيمِ (٣)

*The Most Gracious, the Ever Merciful*

## Important Arabic Words Used In This Verse

***Al* ال; *Rahmân* رحمان; *Rahîm* الرحيم**

***Al-Rahmân* الرحمان and *Al-Rahîm* الرحيم**

**Al** ال: It is equivalent to "The" in English. In Arabic it is used to give the meaning of: Most; All; Complete; Maximum; Whole; Comprehensive; Perfect in all degrees and grades. So Al ال would mean all of the above. [41]

***Al-Rahmân* الرحمان and *Al-Rahîm* الرحيم**: Both these words are both derived from the same root word *Rahima* رَحِمَ. Meanings: Grace; Mercy; Love; Kindness; Tenderness; Forgiveness; Pity; Goodness; Favour; Beneficence. [42 43 44]

***Al-Rahmân***: Derived from the root word *Rahima* رَحِمَ. Meaning: The Most Gracious. The One Who gives without asking and effort.

---

[41] *Dictionary of the Holy Qur'ân by 'Abdul Mannân 'Omar (page 25)*

[42] *Mufradât fi Gharâib al-Qur'ân by Al-Raghib*

[43] *Kashshaf - Commentary by Al- Zamakhsharî*

[44] *Dictionary of the Holy Qur'ân by 'Abdul Mannân 'Omar (page 205)*

It conveys the idea of fullness and extensiveness and indicates the greatest preponderance *(-superiority in weight, power, numbers etc..)* of the quality of grace, love and mercy which comprehends the entire universe without regard to our effort and asking, even before we are born. *Al-Rahmân* is the attribute of Allâh because of His granting to every animate (-being or object having perception and choice), a shape and a constitution appropriate to his or its role.

*Al-Rahmân* bestows upon each one the faculties and powers that are best suited to the life he/it has to live, and equipped each with appropriate bodies and limbs making available to each, all that was suitable and needed for their survival.

*Al-Rahmân* created the celestial bodies and the earth thousands of years before the coming into existence of these creatures, to provide the means of sustenance and protection for them.

*Al-Rahmân* is not contingent on the work and efforts of any creature. It is pure grace, in abundance, which came into effect long before the creation of these beings and objects. *Al-Rahmân* one Who Bestows without reference to effort and without reference to prayer and without distinction between believer and disbeliever. Thus this attribute of Allâh is manifested in both the believer and the unbeliever alike.

*Al-Rahmân* is the source of Love and Mercy in the spiritual life of human beings as well. Allâh's Revelation in the form of Holy Books and Scriptures is an example in this regard. [45]

---

[45] *Dictionary of the Holy Qur'ân by 'Abdul Mannân 'Omar (page 25)*

***Rahîm* رحيم**: Derived from the root word *Rahima* رَحِم. Meanings: Grace; Mercy; Love; Kindness; Tenderness; Forgiveness; Pitty; Goodness; Favour; Beneficence.

*Al-Rahmân* and *Al-Rahîm* are not the repetition of one and the same attribute for the sake of emphasis but are two different attributes. *Al-Rahîm* conveys the meaning of constant repetition and manifestation of this attribute, and giving of liberal reward to those who deserve it and seek of it.

*Al-Rahîm*: Ever Merciful, Ever Loving, and Ever Dispenser of Grace and Love as a result of our deeds and supplications. *Al-Rahîm* causes good results to follow on good deeds and would not nullify and render void anyone's right and virtuous deeds and behavior.

The attribute *Al-Rahmân* circumscribes the quality of 'abounding, rich, and blissful Grace', whereas *Al-Rahîm* the 'continuous manifestation' of Grace and its effect upon us and is a liberal reward of one's deeds and supplications.[46] [47] [48]

[46] *Bahr al-Muhît by Abû Hayyân al-Andulusi*

[47] *Zâd al-Maâd by Ibn Qayyîm*

[48] *Dictionary of the Holy Qur'ân by 'Abdul Mannân 'Omar (page 205-206)*

# Pearls of Wisdom

**The word *Rahmân* has a particular meaning of its own which is not shared by the word *Rahîm*:** By Divine command the beneficence of *Al-Rahmân* has extended to human and animal from time immemorial. This is by virtue of the dictates of Divine Wisdom in accord with the capacity of the recipient and not as a bounty in a uniform measure in all cases. In the operation of this attribute of grace (*Rahmâniyyat*) no effort on the part of human or beast plays any role. It is in fact the pure Grace of Allâh.

It is a universal bounty that proceeds from Allâh, the Most High, which is totally independent of the effort of any imperfect or perfect person.

In short, the grace of *Rahmâniyyat* is not the reward of any one's efforts, nor recognition of any right. On the contrary, it is Allâh's special grace unrelated to obedience or want of it and this grace descends always by the command and will of Allâh, independent of any worship, obedience, righteousness or self-denial. This grace is antecedent to the creation of human and beast and to any effort or supplication on their part. The beneficence of this grace has pervaded through every stage of existence and at all times and places, irrespective of obedience or disobedience.

Do not you see the *Rahmâniyyat (Grace and Beneficence)* of Allâh, the Supreme, extending over both the virtuous and the vicious? The sun and the moon shed their light and luster alike on the saint and the sinner. Allâh has created everything fully equipped with its appropriate faculties and has charged Himself with the affairs of all. There is not a living creature treading the earth or in the heavens but He provides for it. He has grown for them trees, bringing forth fruits, flowers, and fragrance. This is a Mercy that Allâh prepared for His creatures before He created them and in this there is an admonition for the God-fearing. These gifts have been bestowed by Allâh, the Compassionate, the Lord of creation, without reference to any effort or merit.

There are yet other gifts bestowed by the Lord of Majesty which are beyond computation, like the means of sustaining health created by Him and the variety of devices and means of healing for every kind of ailment and the commissioning of Prophets and revelation of Books through Messengers. All this is evidence of the *Rahmâniyyat* (Grace and Beneficence) of our Most Compassionate Lord. This is pure Grace and not in response to the works of a worker, nor in answer to a distress call or a prayer.

***Al-Rahîm* is a special beneficence:** Al-*Rahîm* (Mercy and Compassion) is a special beneficence, distinct from the Grace of *Al-Rahmân* and concerned exclusively with the evolution of the human species and the perfection of human nature. It is contingent upon effort and righteous activity and total suppression of selfish desires.

This aspect of Divine mercy does not manifest itself except in response to the utmost effort in working righteousness and after purification of self and complete sincerity of conduct without the least ostentation and a readiness to suffer death for the sake of winning the pleasure of the Lord of Glory. Truly fortunate are those who become the recipients of these bounties. They are true the Blessed Ones.

"The Arabic words '*Rahmân* and *Rahîm,*' translated 'Most Gracious' and 'Most Merciful' are both intensive forms referring to different aspects of Allah's attribute of Mercy. The Arabic intensive is more suited to express Allah's attributes than the superlative degree in English. The latter implies a comparison with other beings, or with other times or places, while there is no being like unto Allah, and He is independent of Time and Place." [49]

**The revelation of the Holy Word of Allâh is by virtue of this Divine attribute of *Al-Rahmân:*** The revelation of the Holy Word of Allâh and its communication to humanity is by virtue of this Divine attribute of *Rahmâniyyat (Grace and Beneficence).* It is the characteristic of *Rahmâniyyat* that it is manifested on account of pure Divine grace and beneficence, without any reference to any preceding human action and effort.

For instance, the sun, the moon, water, air, matter etc. have all been created for the benefit of humanity by virtue of the Divine attribute of *Rahmâniyyat* and no one can claim that they have been created in consequence of any action or effort on his part. .

The excellent manner in which man's faculties and capacities have been developed and perfected from the beginning is proof of that special grace which is unrelated to any work, worship or effort on the part of man

In the same way the Word of Allâh that came down for the reformation and guidance of humanity owes its genesis to this very attribute. There is not a soul that can claim that the Holy Word of Allâh that comprises the Divine law and

---

[49] *The Meaning of the Holy Qur'ân by 'Abdullah Yûsuf 'Alî, Tenth Edition (page 14)*

guidance was revealed as a reward for any human conduct or effort or his piety or righteousness.

There have been countless pious, spiritual and virtuous people devoted to a life of austerity and worship, but His Holy Word that comprised His commands and injunctions and enlightened His creatures about His purposes, was revealed only by this attribute at certain times when it was most needed.

It is true that the Holy Word of Allâh descends only on those who possess a high degree of purity and righteousness, for the holy and the unholy can have no affinity. But it does not follow that purity and righteousness must be the cause of the descent of the Holy Word.

The revelation of Divine Law and guidance are contingent upon the urgency of the need. Whenever there has been need that the word of Allâh should descend for the reformation of humanity, Allâh, the Lord of Absolute Wisdom, has chosen to send down His word to the person of His choosing and the time of His choosing.

The perfect word of Allâh, comprising Divine law, however, is never sent down at any other time even though there be hundreds of thousands of men possessed of piety, purity and righteousness of a high order.

Of course, many of the righteous are honored with Divine communion (*Wahi-e-Valayt*) by Allâh - which may even assume verbal form, but that also has a purpose, not altogether identical with the purpose which is fulfilled by Divine law and guidance.

The difference is that the revelation of Divine law is needed when the people of the world in consequence of misguidance and the pursuit of erroneous ways depart from the right course and to lead them aright a new law is called for, effective for the purpose of removing their afflictions and dispelling their gloom through the light of its perfect and healing exposition, and to provide the remedy needed to cure the distemper of the age.

But Divine communion with saints (*Wahi-e-Valayt*) is not in response to this great urgency and may be aimed at strengthening the individual in his steadfastness in an hour of tribulation and travail or giving him glad tidings for his good cheer or the like. But the perfect and Holy Word of Allâh that descends on Messengers and Prophets of Allâh, as explained above, is in response to the true need of the human beings for faith and guidance.

In short, true and urgent need is the occasion of the descent of the Divine word, even as when you see darkness enveloping the night entirely with light fading out totally, you perceive the proximity of the appearance of the new moon. In the same way, when utter darkness of misguidance spreads over the earth, inner wisdom perceives the imminence of the appearance of the spiritual new moon.

Similarly, the descent of the Divine word comprising Divine law and guidance is not due to the purity and piety of any individual i.e. the effective cause of its descent is not the extreme piety and purity of any person or his thirst or hunger for righteousness. In fact, as said, the cause of the descent of heavenly guidance is the genuine need for it; the darkness and gloom that envelope the world call for a light, so that it may shine forth to dissipate the darkness.

There is a reference to this in the The Holy Qur'ân:[50]

---

[50] *The Holy Qur'ân: explained by 'Allamah Nooruddîn, rendered into English by Mrs. A. R. 'Omar; 'Abdul Mannân 'Omar*

إِنَّا أَنْزَلْنَاهُ فِي لَيْلَةِ الْقَدْرِ (١)

*'We began to reveal it (-The Qur'ân) during the Night of Majesty' (97:1)*

This night of Majesty is a blessed night in its popular meaning. But the verse just cited also indicates that the darkness of sin prevailing in the world is like the night of Majesty and Determination, because of its hidden beneficent possibilities. During such a period of darkness, sincerity and steadfastness and austerity and worship of Allâh are esteemed highly by Allâh.

It was the same darkness that had reached its darkest pitch at the time of the advent of the Holy Prophet Muhammad (peace and blessings of Allâh be on him), calling for the descent of a glorious-light. It was the black gloom of that darkness that stirred the attribute of *Rahmâniyyat* to compassion for gloom-ridden humanity.

That state of darkness thus became a cause of blessings for the earth and the world experienced, because of it, the most gorgeous manifestation of Divine Mercy in the shape of the Perfect Man, the Seal of the Prophets, Muhammad (pbuh), who had no peer before or after. He came for the guidance of humanity and brought a bright Book, the like of which no human has seen.

It was indeed a great manifestation of God's *Rahmâniyyat* (Gratuitous Grace) that God sent down such a glorious light, the Blessed and Noble Qur'ân, at the time of deepest gloom and darkness, to distinguish between truth and falsehood, which indeed put the truth on top and uprooted falsehood.

The Holy Qur'ân descended on the earth when it was spiritually dead and a great corruption had spread over land

and sea. Through its descent, it brought about the consummation referred to by Allâh in the words: Be sure Allâh revives the earth after its death. It must always be remembered that this descent of the Holy Qur'ân for the spiritual resuscitation of the world took place through a stirring of the attribute of *Rahmâniyyat*.

The Book of God is sent down only when there is a true need for it. In brief, the underlying cause of such Divine revelation is the attribute of *Rahmâniyyat* and, not the virtuous conduct of anyone.

**Allâh is *Al-Rahmân* because of His sheer grace and beneficence and not in return for any one's labor and effort:** Allâh is the *Al-Rahmân* because of His sheer grace and beneficence and not in return for any one's labor and even long before the birth of His creatures and before the commencement of their deeds, He created means of comfort for them, like the sun, the moon, the earth and all the rest. Such bounty is called *Rahmâniyyat* in the Book of Allâh and because of it the Supreme Being is called Al-*Rahmân.*

It is this attribute of *Rahmâniyyat* that, at times, is roused to take care of the famine-stricken and pours out the rain of mercy on parched land and the same attribute is roused to compassion for the spiritually starved and thirsty who are in the death grip of misdirection and misguidance and have run short of the diet of truth and righteousness which is the mainstay of spiritual life.

Look at the system of the universe. There is the sun and there is the moon: there is corn and there is water and air and a variety of herbs to cure us of many ills. Can anyone point to the service rendered by him that earned this return? Whosoever cares to reflect will find that Allâh is *Al-*

*Rahmân.* All that is in the heavens and in the earth and in our bodies owes its origin to His *Rahmâniyyat.*

Allâh says in the Holy Qur'ân:[51]

الرَّحْمٰنُ (١) عَلَّمَ الْقُرْآنَ (٢) خَلَقَ الْإِنْسَانَ (٣) عَلَّمَهُ الْبَيَانَ (٤) الشَّمْسُ وَالْقَمَرُ بِحُسْبَانٍ (٥) وَالنَّجْمُ وَالشَّجَرُ يَسْجُدَانِ (٦) وَالسَّمَاءَ رَفَعَهَا وَوَضَعَ الْمِيزَانَ (٧) أَلَّا تَطْغَوْا فِي الْمِيزَانِ (٨) وَأَقِيمُوا الْوَزْنَ بِالْقِسْطِ وَلَا تُخْسِرُوا الْمِيزَانَ (٩) وَالْأَرْضَ وَضَعَهَا لِلْأَنَامِ (١٠) فِيهَا فَاكِهَةٌ وَالنَّخْلُ ذَاتُ الْأَكْمَامِ (١١) وَالْحَبُّ ذُو الْعَصْفِ وَالرَّيْحَانُ (١٢) فَبِأَيِّ آلَاءِ رَبِّكُمَا تُكَذِّبَانِ (١٣)

*The Most Gracious (God). Has taught this Qur'ân. He created human being; And taught him (the art of) intelligent and distinct speech. The sun and the moon pursue their scheduled courses on their axis according to a fixed reckoning. And the stem-less plants and the trees humbly submit (to His will); And He raised the heaven high and set up the (law of) harmony and balance. (He explains this to you) that you should not violate the (law of) harmony and balance. Hold balance with justice (giving everyone his due avoiding extremes). Do not disturb the (law of) harmony in the least. And He has set the earth for (the common good of) all (His) creatures. In it there are all kinds of fruit and palm-trees (laden) with sheathed clusters, And the grains with the husk-coverings and fragrant flowery plants. Which of the benefactions of your Lord will you twain (believers and disbelievers), then, deny?*
*(55: 1-13)*

[51] *The Holy Qur'ân: explained by 'Allamah Nooruddîn, rendered into English by Mrs. A. R. 'Omar; 'Abdul Mannân 'Omar*

**Al-RA<u>H</u>ÎM رحيم (the Ever Merciful):** Allâh, the Supreme, has two attributes, *Al-Ra<u>h</u>mân and Al-Ra<u>h</u>îm.* He is *Al-Ra<u>h</u>mân*, in the sense that He grants a pure nature to human appropriate for the purpose of seeking Him; and He is *Al-Ra<u>h</u>îm* in the sense that when one employs usefully one's Allâh-given faculties, He blesses one's effort with goodly results.

**Efforts and Striving is essential for achieving good results:** It must be understood that it is through the operation of Allâh's attribute of being Al-*Ra<u>h</u>îm* that a person is enabled to take full advantage of the blessings and benefits of the Divine Word reaching his goal by means of its blessings and light and reaping the harvest of his efforts and diligence.

Allâh says He is the *Ra<u>h</u>îm*, that is, He causes good results to follow on good deeds and would not nullify any one's works. Because of this, He is called *Ra<u>h</u>îm* and this attribute is termed *Ra<u>h</u>îmiyyat.*

That is why in Allâh's Word His attribute of *Ra<u>h</u>îm* is mentioned immediately after His attribute of *Ra<u>h</u>mân* - so that it may be realized that the effectiveness of the Divine Word working upon human souls is brought about by the attribute of *Ra<u>h</u>îmiyyat.*

The more a person discard inner and outer indifference and disinclination, and the deeper he grows in sincerity and righteousness and the closer he approaches to obedience of his Creator Allâh through effort and application, the stronger is the impact of the Divine Word on his heart and in like proportion does he derive benefit from its lights and cultivates in himself the characteristics of those who are acceptable to Allâh.

For seeking the benefit of *Rahîmiyyat* it is incumbent on a person to strive. That is why God has assured us:[52]

وَالَّذِينَ جَاهَدُوا فِينَا لَنَهْدِيَنَّهُمْ سُبُلَنَا ۚ وَإِنَّ اللَّـهَ لَمَعَ الْمُحْسِنِينَ (٦٩)

*'And those who strive hard in Our cause We will certainly guide them in the ways that lead to Us. Verily, Allâh is always with the doers of good'. (29.69)*

The meaning of *Al-Rahîm* is that Allâh, the Supreme, causes good results to follow upon good deeds. As, for example, the one who offers Prayer, observes fast for Him, bestows in charity, is rewarded and shown mercy in this world and the next.

Allâh says: Allâh does not let go waste the effort of those who do good. Allâh says in the Holy Qur'ân: [53]

فَمَنْ يَعْمَلْ مِثْقَالَ ذَرَّةٍ خَيْرًا يَرَهُ (٧)

*'Then whosoever has done so much as an atom's weight of good will see (the good results of it). (99:7)*

**Whatever has to be shall be and that it is no use bothering about anything:** Allah is *Al-Rahîm*, that is, He requites deeds. There are some who declare good works are superfluous. They have no use for prayers and fasting and say that if fortune favors them they will escape all ill. In other words, their attitude is whatever has to be shall be and that it is no use bothering about anything.

The most ignorant share this ill-founded view. They leave everything to fate. They say they are not aspiring to be

[52] *The Holy Qur'ân: explained by 'Allamah Nooruddîn, rendered into English by Mrs. A. R. 'Omar; 'Abdul Mannân 'Omar*

[53] *ibid*

saints that they should subject themselves to hardships. But Allâh says: I am *Al-Rahîm.* I will promote to high ranks those who act righteously and are devoted out of sincere love for Him. The seeker finds, the one who endures hardship is always rewarded. Thus the attribute *Al-Rahîm* rebukes those who say that what is decreed must come to pass and that, therefore, worship is superfluous. That is why Allah has assured us:[54]

وَالَّذِينَ جَاهَدُوا فِينَا لَنَهْدِيَنَّهُمْ سُبُلَنَا ۚ وَإِنَّ اللَّهَ لَمَعَ الْمُحْسِنِينَ (٦٩)

*'And those who strive hard in Our cause We will certainly guide them in the ways that lead to Us. Verily, Allâh is always with the doers of good'. (29.69)*

Yes, all the saints and the rignteous endured privations before this door opened to them. Allâh is *Al-Rahîm*, that is, He causes good results to follow upon appropriate effort.

For instance, a peasant cultivates his land and irrigates it. Now, as the way of Allâh is, He does not render vain the work of anyone. Indeed He bestows many grains in return for a single one. The crop might fail due to some hidden default or the wrong ways of the cultivator, but this is seldom. Hence we should always ask for help and guidance from Allâh – so as to reach our noble and virtuous goals.

**Rahîmiyyat stimulates hope and effort:** Allâh has mentioned *Al-Rahîm (the Ever Merciful)* as His attribute in the rest of the Holy Qur'ân as well. This means that He does not let go waste any one's work or effort. Indeed, He crowns them with results and achievement. If a person did not believe that his labor and his work would produce

[54] *The Holy Qur'ân: explained by 'Allamah Nooruddîn, rendered into English by Mrs. A. R. 'Omar; 'Abdul Mannân 'Omar*

results, he would grow indifferent and lazy. Thus this attribute *Al-Rahîm* widens the horizon of human hope and acts as a powerful incentive towards good-deeds.

It would be borne in mind that in the language of the Holy Qur'ân, Allâh, the Most High, is called *Al-Rahîm (The Ever Merciful)* in the sense that He hears the prayers and supplications of His creatures and accepts their good deeds and averts calamities and visitations and does not let go waste their works in His cause. Whenever we put in hard work in conformity with Divine laws, in pursuit of a temporal or a religious objective, we find Divine mercy attending us instantly, making our labor fruitful.

*Rahîmiyyat* is the one that comes into operation in consequence of man's virtuous effort. When he prays with humility his prayer is heard. When he cultivates his land with diligence the Divine mercy blesses the seed, so that a large quantity of grain is produced. Reflection would show that Divine mercy attends all our efforts, whether they be mundane or spiritual.

*Rahîmiyyat* رحيميت: *(Compassion and Mercy)* is concerned exclusively with humans - other creatures have not been granted the capacity for prayer, supplication and virtuous deeds. Human alone has been so endowed.

Thus the difference between *Rahmâniyyat* and *Rahîmiyyat* is that the former does not call for prayer/deeds, and the latter does.

*Rahmâniyyat* is 'Grace' that started long before our coming into existence. For instance, Allâh visualizing through His eternal knowledge created the kind of earth and heaven and earthly and heavenly objects that could be of use to His creatures and are used by us. It is a human who derives the utmost benefit from these objects.

*Al-Rahmân* created the necessary elements and other objects prior to our birth which are constantly serving us. These are due to the urge of *Rahmâniyyat,* antecedent to our existence, longing, or even our prayer.

The second type of mercy is due to *Rahîmiyyat* -when we pray and do righteous deeds, Allâh the Supreme bestows the reward. A little reflection will show that the law of nature is linked to prayer and righteous deeds.

**Keep in mind the relationship between the baby and its mother when pondering the philosophy of prayer:** When a baby cries and yells for milk in the grip of hunger, milk suddenly surges up in the mother's breasts. The baby has not the least idea of prayer. How then do his cries draw milk so close to him? This is a matter of common experience. It is often the case that the mother does not even perceive the presence of milk in her breasts but the cries and moans of the baby suddenly draw it up.

By the same token then will our cries unto Allâh, the Exalted, fail to draw anything? Certainly not. Indeed, every boon is granted. Only those lacking insight, the self-styled savants and philosophers fail to perceive it. If one keeps in mind the relationship between the baby and its mother when pondering the philosophy of prayer, one will find it easy to comprehend it.

Prayer is a human characteristic and responding to prayer is a Divine attribute. He who will not understand and will not believe clings to falsehood. The illustration of the child and the mother that is cited helps to understand the philosophy of prayer.

This kind of mercy teaches the lesson that compassion of this type is induced only by prayer. Ask and you will be given. Call on Me, I shall respond to you. The Holy Qur'ân says:[55]

وَكَأَيِّنْ مِنْ دَابَّةٍ لَا تَحْمِلُ رِزْقَهَا اللَّـهُ يَرْزُقُهَا وَإِيَّاكُمْ ۚ وَهُوَ السَّمِيعُ الْعَلِيمُ (٦٠)

*'And your Rabb (Lord) says, 'Call on Me, I will answer your prayer...' (40.60)*

*Al-Ra<u>h</u>mân* and Al-*Ra<u>h</u>îm* are not completely separated one from the other. *Ra<u>h</u>mâniyyat* by its very nature invests us with the capacity to avail ourselves of the mercy of *Ra<u>h</u>îmiyyat*. He who does not recognize this law of Allah and does not avail this opportunity, lacks gratitude for the bounties bestowed through *Ra<u>h</u>mâniyyat*.

**Understanding of Allah's Worship:** "Worshiping Allâh", means we serve and worship Thee through utilizing all the means and material which Allâh hast granted us through his attribute of <u>*Al-Rahmân*</u>.

Remember, therefore, that if we make supplication without making proper use, at the same time, of our faculties and capacities and putting them into use and action, such prayer alone can be of no avail. Since we did not make use of the divine bounties already bestowed on us, how can we expect to derive benefit through another, namely prayer.

Consider the gift of the tongue that is composed of nerves and muscles. If that were not so we would not be capable of speech or utterance. He granted us a tongue for prayer that could effcctively express the thoughts of the mind. If we stop making use of the tongue for prayer that would be our misfortune.

---

*[55] The Holy Qur'ân: explained by 'Allamah Nooruddîn, rendered into English by Mrs. A. R. 'Omar; 'Abdul Mannân 'Omar*

The faculties of a person afflicted with madness are rendered inoperative. Should we not, then, appreciate our Allâh-given bounties? If we neglect the faculties and capacities that Allâh, the Supreme, has bestowed upon us through His perfect grace and beneficence, we would be guilty of ingratitude.

These two kinds of mercy *Rahmâniyyat* and *Rahîmiyyat* are indispensable for our very existence. Can any one question their existence? Indeed not. In truth they are the most evident manifestations that keep the whole system of our lives running.

**His two attributes, in two forms for the fostering of our existence - in the laws of nature:** Now then, when it is clear that for our growth and evolution the Almighty had set running the two springs of two Mercies which, in fact, are His two attributes, in two forms for the fostering of our existence we should try to discover how they are designated in the Qur'ânic language.

Know then that in respect of the first kind of mercy, Allâh the Supreme has been named *Al-Rahmân* in Arabic and in respect of the second kind of mercy He is named Al-*Rahîm*, in the Arabic language. This shows that since this attribute of mercy was divided into two categories of Divine Law from the beginning, there are two basic words in Arabic to convey their meaning.

It will be a very instructive method for a seeker after truth to take from the attributes and works of Allâh so manifest in the chronicle of nature, a cue for discovering the subtle differences in the meanings of Qur'ânic words, and to look for their distinguishing characteristics as demonstrated in the operation of the laws of nature in the basic words of the Qur'ânic language.

Wherever it is desired to demonstrate the distinction, between the signification of two Arabic synonyms which have reference to Divine attributes or works of Allah, one should turn to the division of Divine attributes or Divine works as illustrated in the laws of nature. For, the real purpose of Arabic is to convey knowledge of the Divine as the purpose of the creation of a human is that he should know Allâh. And the best way to know the properties and the essence of an object is to keep its purpose in mind.

These two attributes, *Al-Rahmân* and *Al-Rahîm*, are indispensible for a successful prosecution of temporal as well as spiritual undertakings. A little reflection would show that both these attributes are in operation incessantly for the consummation of all projects in the world.

Allâh's *Rahmâniyyat* has been in operation from long before the advent of a human being. It is this attribute of Allâh that provides human with means and resources that lie far beyond his power and beyond the range of human action and human planning to secure. Nor are these means and resources the reward of any human effort. They are bounties bestowed as pure Grace and Benevolence.

As for instance, rainfall, the sun, the moon, the air and the clouds, all carrying out their allotted functions and so also the advent of humans in this world equipped with appropriate faculties and capacities and endowed with good health, security, leisure and life. Most importantly, the advent of Prophets, the revelation of Books All these are manifestations of the attribute of *Rahmâniyyat*.

In contrast, the Divine attribute of *Rahîmiyyat* manifests itself when a person puts in motion his Allâh-given faculties for the attainment of a certain objective and expends all the energy, vigor and strength that he can muster to that end, then, Allâh, as is His way, does not let his effort go waste and crowns it with the best result. It is indeed the sheer *Ra<u>h</u>îmiyyat* of Allâh that infuses life into the lifeless efforts of a person.

When we study the Divine Law of nature, we clearly discern that whatever Allâh has provided for His servants is divisible in two kinds. One consists of His bounties which precede the coming into existence of human and have nothing whatever to do with any effort on his part. For instance, He made the sun, the moon, the stars, the earth, water, air and fire for the well-being and comfort of humans. They preceded the coming into existence of humans and his deeds. Indeed a human came into being long after their emergence. This is the type of Divine mercy which is called *Ra<u>h</u>mâniyyat* in the language of the Holy Qur'ân. It is a bounty that is not bestowed in return for a person's virtuous deeds but is bestowed by way of pure Grace and Beneficence.

The other kind of mercy is termed *Rahîmiyyat* in the language of the Holy Qur'ân, that is, the rewards and bounties that are bestowed on human in return for his virtuous deeds. Allâh is *Al-Ra<u>h</u>îm* - He rewards the honest labor and diligence of human beings. A person puts in honest hard work. The way of Allâh is that He would not let honest labor and hard work, go waste. Instead He invests it with good results.

The distinction between *Ra<u>h</u>mân and Ra<u>h</u>îm* is that the former is unrelated to action and effort while the latter is contingent on them; but there is the possibility of human failure. **Divine compassion seeks to cover it.**

**Allâh made available to all that was needed and suitable for their survival - for birds, beasts and the humans:** The Divine attribute which may be termed general beneficence, is called *Rahmâniyyat* by virtue of which Allâh is named *Al-Rahmân. Al-Rahmân* is the attribute of Allâh because of His granting to every animate, including human, a shape and a constitution appropriate to his or its role, i.e. He bestowed upon each one the faculties and powers that are best suited to the life it has to live, and equipped each with appropriate bodies and limbs making available to each all that was needed for their survival, for the birds and the beasts and for humans, all that was suitable.

Not only that, He created the celestial bodies and the earth thousands of years before the coming into existence of these creatures, to provide the means of sustenance and protection for them.

This shows that the *Rahmâniyyat* of Allâh, the Supreme, is not contingent on the work of any creature; it is, in fact, pure grace which came into operation long before the creation of these objects. A human being enjoys the largest share of this beneficence, for everything serves to promote his welfare. That is why every human has been reminded that his God is *Al-Rahmân.*

***Al-Rahîm* is the special grace exclusively for humans:** Allâh, the Most High, is called *Al-Rahîm* according to the Holy Qur'ân, when He accepts the prayers, humble supplications and good deeds of men and women and safeguards them against calamities and afflictions and loss of the fruits of their labors.

This beneficence is called special grace because it has relation exclusively to humans. Allâh has not bestowed upon other animals the faculty of prayer and supplication or of righteous action. Only a human has been endowed with this faculty. A human possesses the faculty of speech and is thus capable of attracting Divine grace by means of his/her supplications. Other creatures have not been endowed with that faculty.

It should, therefore, be obvious that Prayer is a characteristic of human nature, having been embedded in it. Just as grace is received through the Divine attributes of Providence *(Rabûbiyyat)* and Beneficence and Graciousness *(Ra<u>h</u>mâniyyat),* so is one kind of grace received through the Divine attribute of *Ra<u>h</u>îmiyyat*, the only difference being that for *Rabûbiyyat* (Providence) and *Ra<u>h</u>mâniyyat* (Graciousness) prayer or action is not a prerequisite, because, both these attributes are not related exclusively to humanity but are shared by with beasts and birds and other parts of Allah's creation.

For instance, the attribute *Rabûbiyyat (Providence)* benefits all animates, vegetables and minerals and all earthly and celestial bodies, not a single object being beyond the orbit of its benevolence, unlike the Divine attribute *Ra<u>h</u>îmiyyat* which is the exclusive privilege of humans. If human fails to avail himself of this attribute, he degrades himself to the level of beasts, even lower.

Out of His four attributes of Beneficence, Allâh has reserved one, *Ra<u>h</u>îmiyyat*, exclusively for humans, and this attribute calls for prayer and supplication and righteous deeds. It is thus emphasized that a particular type of grace is bestowed only in answer to prayer, supplication and righteous deeds and is not attainable through any other means.

This is the way and law of Allâh admitting of no variation. It was because of this that all the Prophets (peace be upon them) were constant in their prayers and supplications on behalf of their followers. Read the Torah and you will find how often the children of Israel were threatened with

Divine affliction for their having offended Allâh, but the punishment was averted through the prayers, supplications and prostrations of Moses, though time and again Allâh had threatened to destroy them.

**Prayer and Supplication is not a meaningless form of worship:** All this shows that prayer is not a meaningless form of worship that does not attract any kind of grace. This is the view of those who do not esteem Allâh as highly as He is entitled to be esteemed, nor do they ponder over His word deeply, nor do they study the laws of nature.

The truth is that prayer indeed attracts the grace that saves us and is named *Rahîmiyyat*, impelling humans towards continuous progress. It is by means of this grace that a true worshipper reaches the stage in which Allâh becomes his guardian, his faith, acquiring the quality whereby he believes in Allâh with such certainty as if he sees Him with his own eyes.

# VERSE 4

مَالِكِ يَوْمِ الدِّينِ

Master of the Day of Requital

## Important Arabic Words Used In This Verse

***Mâlik* مالک; *Youm* یوم; *Dîn* دین**

*Mâlik* مالک; *(Root Word: Malaka* مَلَکَ*):*

**Meanings:** Master and Sovereign Authority; Severing; Lord; Owner; Possessor; Ruler; King; Reign; Dominion; Authority; Take a wife; Hold; Power to Prevail; Capable.
*Mâlik* مالک and *Malik* ملک are two different words from the same root *(Malaka* مَلَکَ)

Who possesses the Sovereign and complete right of ownership over a thing and has the power to deal with it as one likes. The adoption of the word *Mâlik* (Master and Sovereign Authority) is to show that Allâh has the supreme authority to forgive and/or reward multiple times. Allâh is not guilty of injustice if He forgives his worshippers, because He is not a mere king or a mere judge, but more properly a Master and Sovereign Authority. [56] [57]

## Youm يوم: (Root Word يوم Yauma)

**Meanings**: Day; Time; Day of a Battle; Day and Night; Moment; Aeon (- an immeasurably long period of time); Space of Time; Thousand Years; Fifty Thousand Years. [58]

## Dîn دين: (Root word Dâna دان)

**Meanings:** Requital; Judgment; Faith; Recompense; Religion; Law; Religious Laws; Obedience; Be Honored, Be Revealed; Management; Debt; Credit; Transact; Reckoning; Customs; Victory; Government; Power; Affair…[59]

*Al-Dîn* الدين: the Requital (-The actual execution of the Judgment).

[56] *Dictionary of the Holy Qur'ân by 'Abdul Mannân 'Omar (page 540-541)*
[57] *Bahr al-Muhît by Abû Hayyân al-Andulusi*
[58] *Dictionary of the Holy Qur'ân by 'Abdul Mannân 'Omar (page 628)*
[59] *Dictionary of the Holy Qur'ân by 'Abdul Mannân 'Omar (page 185)*

# Pearls of Wisdom

In describing Allâh, as 'Master of the Day of Requital', the Holy Qur'ân lays stress on the fact that the Divine Law of Requital of Deeds is working every moment, and thus makes human being feel the responsibility of their actions.

It can be considered as 'the law of motivation'. It is only the awe of Divine Majesty that can safeguard against sin. Once we realize that we are responsible for our action, and Allâh is *Mâlik e- Youmidîn* 'Dispenser of Reward and Punishment'. This consciousness would become a positive motivation for virtuous deeds and barrier against sin.

*Mâlik e- Youmidîn* does not signify that reward and punishment will be awarded only in the hereafter. The Holy Qur'ân makes it clear that there is a continuous judgment and requital in this very life as well.

Yes The Holy Qur'ân also makes it clear that the Day of Requital is the "Day of the Greatest Dispensation". 'The Reward' or 'The Punishment' will be manifested in its purest form, on the ultimate 'Day of Requital'.

***Mâlik e- Youmiddîn* (Supreme and Sovereign Master of the time of Requital) - the fourth category of Divine Beneficence:** The fourth category of Divine beneficence, mentioned in this fourth verse, is Allah's fourth grace which has been termed the most exclusive beneficence. It is distinguished from the attribute *Rahîmiyyat* in that under *Rahîmiyyat* through prayer, supplication and righteous deeds the worshipper is deemed worthy of grace, but it is through the attribute *Mâlik e Youmiddîn* that the grace is bestowed.

For example, a student through diligent application and hard work learns the law of the land and passes the prescribed test in it. Qualifying for success through the blessings of *Rahîmiyyat* is akin to passing an examination; attaining the objective or the position for which one has qualified is akin to attaining the grace awarded by virtue of the attribute *Mâlik e- Youmiddîn* (the absolute Divine over lordship on the day and time of requital).

These two attributes, *Rahîmiyyat* and *Mâlikiyyat e-Youmiddîn* indicate that the beneficence of *Rahîmiyyat* accrues from the Mercy and Compassion of Allâh, the Supreme. And the beneficence of *Mâlikiyyat e-Youmiddîn* accrues from the grace of the Supreme Lord, and though the latter will make its full manifestation in the hereafter.

These four attributes of Allâh – *Rabb; Al-Rahmân; Al-Rahîm; Mâlik e-Youmiddîn* are constantly operative in this realm of earthly existence, within the limits of its sphere. *Rabubiyyat* (Providence – Divine Lordship) as a general rule, sows the seed of one kind of beneficence, *Rahmâniyyat* extends that beneficence manifestly to all animates, while *Rahîmiyyat* shows humans at the terminal end of the elongated line of beneficence. Human is a being who does not ask for grace but only through his prayer, conduct and condition. *Mâlikiyyat e- Youmiddîn* grants the final reward of grace.

**In the hereafter these four attributes shall appear in full display:** These four attributes are in operation in this life. But as the sphere of earthly existence is narrow and since a human is handicapped by ignorance, unawareness and shortsightedness, the immensely extensive spheres of these four attributes appears small as viewed from this life, as do the big spheres of stars like dots from a long distance.

In the hereafter, however, these four attributes shall appear in full display and thus the true and perfect Judgment and Requital Day will be manifested in the hereafter. There the operation of each of these attributes will be displayed two fold, both manifestly and covertly. These four attributes will thus appear as eight. It is this phenomenon that has been described in the Divine Word that eight angels will uphold the Divine Throne on that Day whereas four are upholding it here. [60]

وَالْمَلَكُ عَلَىٰ أَرْجَائِهَا ۚ وَيَحْمِلُ عَرْشَ رَبِّكَ فَوْقَهُمْ يَوْمَئِذٍ ثَمَانِيَةٌ (١٧)

*And the angels will be (standing) on all sides (of the heaven) and eight (divine powers) will on that day be above them bearing the Throne of Power of your Lord. (69:17)*

This is a figure of speech. Since an angel has been created to attend on each Divine attribute, therefore, four angels have been mentioned as attending on four attributes. When eight attributes are manifested, they will be attended by eight angels and since they uphold the nature of Divine attributes in such a manner as if they were sustaining them, they are figuratively supporting them. Such delicate figures of speech abound in the Word of God, interpreting the spiritual realm in terms of physical life.

*Mâlik e-Youmiddîn* means that all recompense is in Allâh's hands. He has not withdrawn Himself from the governance of the universe committing it to some vicegerent with all authority to award recompense here and hereafter.

---

[60] *The Holy Qur'ân: explained by 'Allamah Nooruddîn, rendered into English by Mrs. A. R. 'Omar; 'Abdul Mannân 'Omar*

The word *Mâlik* (Supreme Sovereign/ Complete Master) negatives all rights in the subject. It is applicable in its fullest meaning to Allâh alone, for He alone is the complete Master. One who acknowledges someone as the master of his life and substance affirms that he himself has no right whatsoever over his life and property and that everything belongs to the master *(Mâlik)* – Allâh.

**To punish every default is incompatible with the Divine attributes of forgiveness:** To punish every default is incompatible with the Divine attributes of forgiveness and forbearance. He is the Master *(Mâlik)* and not a mere magistrate or judge. He has named Himself *Mâlik* (Complete Master), in the phrase *Mâlik e-Youmiddîn*, meaning that He has full authority to dispense reward and punishment. It is obvious that no one can be truly called Master *(Mâlik)* unless he has the sovereign power to punish or pardon as he may determine.

This world is a realm of trial. For its consequences and recompense there is another realm. Allâh has promised happiness in the hereafter in recompense for the hardships endured in this world. If someone questions His dispensation, the answer is that He possesses complete dominion and complete mastery. He does as He wills. There is no room for anyone to find fault with that which He does.

It is only the awe of Divine Majesty that can safeguard against sin. Once one realizes that God is *Mâlik e-Youmiddîn* - Dispenser of reward and punishment, and that His punishment is severe and His reward is bountiful, that awesome consciousness would become a barrier against sin, and a motivation for being virtuous.[61]

---

[61] *The Holy Qur'ân: explained by 'Allamah Nooruddîn, rendered into English by Mrs. A. R. 'Omar; 'Abdul Mannân 'Omar*

يَا أَيُّهَا الَّذِينَ آمَنُوا إِنْ تَتَّقُوا اللَّـهَ يَجْعَلْ لَكُمْ فُرْقَانًا وَيُكَفِّرْ عَنْكُمْ سَيِّئَاتِكُمْ وَيَغْفِرْ لَكُمْ ۗ وَاللَّـهُ ذُو الْفَضْلِ الْعَظِيمِ (٢٩)

***O** you who believe! if you take Allâh as a shield He will grant you Discrimination (between right and wrong) and rid you of all your evil thoughts and deeds, and will protect you (against their adverse consequences), for Allâh is Possessor of great bounties. (8:29)*

**Besides the day of greatest Dispensation there is continuous judgment in this life as well:** *Mâlike Youmiddîn* (Supreme Master of the Day of Requital) does not signify that reward and punishment will be awarded only in the hereafter. The Holy Qur'ân makes it clear that the Day of Requital is the Day of the Greatest Dispensation and that there is a continuous judgment and requital in this life also.

We have observed that whosoever is steadfast in virtue is not left without his reward and that he who does evil suffers evil. For example, adultery and homosexuality invites venereal disease and drunkenness brings on palsy or ulcers and/or other health related, social and economic problems.

*Mâlik e-Youmiddîn* (Supreme Master of the Day of Requital) refutes those who do not believe in resurrection. This has been explained in detail in several places in the Holy Qur'ân. The difference between this Divine attribute and *Ra<u>h</u>îmiyyat* is that *Ra<u>h</u>îmiyyat* opens the way to success through prayer, worship and virtuous acts and deeds whereby a reward is earned and *Mâlik e-Youmiddîn* <u>confers</u> that reward.

**Allâh's manifests Himself in four primary ways, why did Allâh adopt that sequence and order of mentioning His four attributes?** As we have read so far, that in Surah *Al-Fâti<u>h</u>ah*, Allâh, the Exalted, has set forth His four principal attributes. Namely: *Rabbil'Âlamîn; Al -Ra<u>h</u>mâ*; *Al-Ra<u>h</u>îm; Mâlik e-Youmiddîn.*

Giving priority to the attribute *Rabbil-'Âlamîn* and setting out *Al-Ra<u>h</u>mân, Al-Rahîm, Mâlik e- Youmiddîn* thereafter in that order.

Now why did Allâh, the Exalted, adopt that sequence and order? The answer is that that is their natural order, because these four attributes come into operation in that sequence and order in the entire domain and Kingdom of Allâh. For example:

**The first attribute of *Rabb -'Âlamîn*:** *It* is the most universal. An intelligent observer can discover for himself that Allâh's grace manifests itself in the world in four ways. The first is the most universal, that absolute benevolence which continually embraces and supports every animate and inanimate object from the highest heaven to the earth.

The very coming into being of each thing from non-existence and its maturity into perfection is through the operation of this grace and no animate or inanimate object is outside its purview. All bodies and souls owe their existence to it, and everything receives its sustenance through it. This grace is the very breath of life of the entire universe. Were it cut off for one moment, the entire universe would perish. But for it nothing of creation would have come into existence. It has been termed *Rabubiyyat* in the Holy Qur'ân and it is on its account that Allâh has been called *Rabbil-'Âlamîn*, the Lord of Universal Providence, Guardian Sustainer and Evolver to Perfection.

As has been said in another place in the Holy Qur'ân: [62]

قُلْ أَغَيْرَ اللَّـهِ أَبْغِي رَبًّا وَهُوَ رَبُّ كُلِّ شَيْءٍ ۚ

*Say, 'Shall I seek a Lord other than Allâh whilst He is the Lord of all things?' ... (6.164)*

*Al-Hamdu lillahe Rabbil-'Âlamîn* (all perfect and true praise is due to the Lord of Universal Providence alone). That is so, both because in the natural order the attribute of providence comes into operation before the other Divine attributes of beneficence and also because it is the most comprehensive, covering as it does everything, animate and inanimate.

**The second attribute of *Al-Rahmân*:** The next in order is the second category of grace is the grace of ***Rahmân**iyyat* which is general, the difference between the two being that the first attribute (***Rabbûbiyat***) is an all-embracing Providence by means of which the entire creation came into being and continues to be sustained and the latter (*Rahmâniyyat*) is a special eternal grace which extends only to the animates.

In other words, the special concern of the Divine for the entire animal kingdom has been called (*Rahmâniyyat*). The characteristic of this grace is that it extends to all members of the animal kingdom without reference to any merit or right of any of them, in proportion to their respective requirements, not being the recompense of any action on their part.

It is because of this *Rahmâniyyat* grace that every sentient being is alive, works, eats, drinks, feels secure against

[62] *The Holy Qur'ân: explained by 'Allamah Nooruddîn, rendered into English by Mrs. A. R. 'Omar; 'Abdul Mannân 'Omar*

afflictions, and has his needs fulfilled. It is because of this grace that all the requirements of life for every animate and for the survival of its species have been made available.

It is by the blessing of this grace that all that is needed for physical development has been provided and all that is needed for spiritual development by those who are gifted with spiritual faculties has also been provided from the earliest times, according to their needs, through Divine revelation.

In short through this grace of *Rahmâniyyat* a human enjoys the fulfillment of millions of his wants. For his habitation there is the surface of the earth, for light there are the sun and the moon, for breathing there is air, for drinking there is water, for eating there is a large variety of foodstuffs, for treatment of ills and ailments there are innumerable drugs and remedies, for wearing there are different kinds of apparel and for guidance there are Divine scriptures.

No one can claim that these are the consequences of his actions or that he had been engaged in some virtuous pursuit in a previous incarnation in appreciation of which God has bestowed all these innumerable bounties upon humanity.

It is thus established that this grace (*Rahmâniyyat)* which manifests itself in thousands of ways for promoting the wellbeing of all animates is a gratuitous bounty unrelated to any action on the part of anyone. It is but the upsurge of Divine mercy so that every animate creature may attain his natural goal and may satisfy the urges inherent in his nature. The function of eternal bounty as manifested through this grace is to provide for the needs of all living creatures and to look after all that is good for them and that is harmful for them lest they perish or their capacities stay dormant.

The Divine Being possesses this attribute *Rahmâniyyat* is manifestly established through a study of the law of nature. No sensible person would dispute the fact that all these objects like the sun, the moon, the earth and the elements that are the mainstay of life proceed from this very grace and that every animate, man and beast, believer and disbeliever, good and bad, is benefiting there from, according to his needs and not a single animate being is excluded from their scope.

This grace is called *Rahmâniyyat* in the Holy Qur'ân and by virtue of it the attribute *Rahmân* is mentioned in Surah *Al-Fâtihah* immediately after *Rabbil-'Alamîn.*

This attribute is mentioned at several other places also in the Holy Qur'ân. [63]

وَإِذَا قِيلَ لَهُمُ اسْجُدُوا لِلرَّحْمَٰنِ قَالُوا وَمَا الرَّحْمَٰنُ أَنَسْجُدُ لِمَا تَأْمُرُنَا وَزَادَهُمْ نُفُورًا ۩ (٦٠) تَبَارَكَ الَّذِي جَعَلَ فِي السَّمَاءِ بُرُوجًا وَجَعَلَ فِيهَا سِرَاجًا وَقَمَرًا مُنِيرًا (٦١) وَهُوَ الَّذِي جَعَلَ اللَّيْلَ وَالنَّهَارَ خِلْفَةً لِمَنْ أَرَادَ أَنْ يَذَّكَّرَ أَوْ أَرَادَ شُكُورًا (٦٢)

*And when it is said to them, `Prostrate (to show submission) to the Most Gracious (God).' They say, `What (thing) is this the Most Gracious (God)? Shall we prostrate to whatever you bid us to show submission?' So this (bidding of the Prophet to submit to the Lord) increased them in aversion (to the truth).*

***B**lessed is He Who has placed stars in the heaven and has set in it the glowing sun (that produces light) and the glittering moon (that reflects light).*

---

[63] *The Holy Qur'ân: explained by 'Allamah Nooruddîn, rendered into English by Mrs. A. R. 'Omar; 'Abdul Mannân 'Omar*

*And it is He Who has made the night and the day, one following the other; (He has done it) for (the benefit of) the person who would care to receive exhortation and who would care to be grateful. (25:60-62)*

When the disbelievers are invited to submit themselves to *Al-Rahmân*, they declare their aversion in the retort: Who is this *Al-Rahmân*? Shall we submit to whatever you say? Tell them: *Al-Rahmân* is that source of blessings and of perpetual good, Who has made mansions in the heaven and has placed therein the sun as a lamp and the moon shedding luster for all without discrimination between believer and disbeliever: that *Al-Rahmân* made for you, that is, for the whole of humanity, day and night that alternate so that a seeker of insight may be instructed by the wisdom underlying the system and be relieved from the darkness of ignorance and neglect and he who is disposed to be grateful may' render thanks for Divine bounties.

The true worshippers of *Al-Rahmân* are those who walk on the earth in humility and when the ignorant accost them roughly they answer back gently: Peace. In thus turning away wrath with gentleness and pronouncing blessings in return for vilification they reflect the Divine attribute of *Rahmâniyyat*, as the *Al-Rahmân* pours forth His grace on all His creatures, without discrimination of good and bad, through the sun, the moon, the earth and other innumerable bounties.

Thus Allâh, the Exalted, has made it clear that He is *Al-Rahmân*, in the sense that His mercy extends to everyone, good and bad, without distinction. The same concept is expressed in the Holy Qur'ân: [64]

---

[64] *The Holy Qur'ân: explained by 'Allamah Nooruddîn, rendered into English by Mrs. A. R. 'Omar; 'Abdul Mannân 'Omar*

قُلْ مَنْ يَكْلَؤُكُمْ بِاللَّيْلِ وَالنَّهَارِ مِنَ الرَّحْمَٰنِ ۗ بَلْ هُمْ عَنْ ذِكْرِ رَبِّهِمْ مُعْرِضُونَ (٤٢)

*Say, `Who can protect you by night and in the daytime from (the punishment of) the Most Gracious (God)?' But rather (than thank Him) they are (truly) averse to proclaiming the greatness of their Lord. (21:42)*

That is to say, it is because of Him being *Al Rahmân* that He gives respite to the disbelievers and the disobedient, that they may have the opportunity to repent, and does not seize them quickly.

In *Ch.67:Verse19* also, attention is drawn to His *Rahmâniyyat:* Ask the disbelievers and the disobedient: Have they not observed the birds flying above, spreading out their wings and then drawing them in? It is *Al-Rahmân* who keeps them from falling. [65]

أَوَلَمْ يَرَوْا إِلَى الطَّيْرِ فَوْقَهُمْ صَافَّاتٍ وَيَقْبِضْنَ ۚ مَا يُمْسِكُهُنَّ إِلَّا الرَّحْمَٰنُ ۚ إِنَّهُ بِكُلِّ شَيْءٍ بَصِيرٌ (١٩)

*Have they not seen above them the birds with spread out wings (in flight) which they also draw in (to swoop down on the prey). None but the Most Gracious (God) holds them (there). Verily, He has knowledge of each and everything. (67:19)*

In other words, the grace of *Rahmâniyyat* is so comprehensive that even the birds sail joyfully and happily in the vast expanse of its beneficence.

Since this grace is next in order after *Rububiyyat* (universal providence), Allâh, the Exalted, has mentioned His

[65] *The Holy Qur'ân: explained by 'Allamah Nooruddîn, rendered into English by Mrs. A. R. 'Omar; 'Abdul Mannân 'Omar*

attribute *Al-Rahmân* immediately after His attribute *Rabbil-'Âlamîn*, to preserve the natural order between them.

**The Third attribute of *Al-Rahîm*:** The third category of grace ***Rahîm**iyyat* is the special benevolence. The distinction between this and general benevolence ***Rahmân**iyyat* is that it is not required of the recipient of general benevolence to conform his conduct to virtue or to pull himself out of the grip of dark barriers or to exert himself and put in any particular effort. On the contrary, Allâh, the Exalted, extends this grace to every animate to the extent of his requirement, without supplication or effort on his part.

But for special benevolence of *Al-Rahîm*, effort, exertion, purification of heart, prayer and supplication and earnest direction of the mind towards Allâh and every kind of appropriate striving are necessary conditions. It is only one who earnestly seeks this grace who receives it. It attends only those who work hard for it.

This special grace of *Al-Rahîm* is also comprehended through a study of the law of nature. It is obvious that those who strive in the way of Allâh and those who are indifferent towards it cannot be equal. Those who strive in the way of Allâh, with a sincere heart, and keep away from every kind of evil and mischief, become recipients of this special grace from *Al-Rahim*.

Because the attribute of being *Al-Rahîm* is exclusive and conditional it ranks after the attribute of being *Al- Rahmân. Rahmâniyyat* came into operation first and *Rahîmiyyat* followed it and it was because of this natural order that it was mentioned after the attribute *Rahmâniyyat* in *Surah Al-Fâtihah* in the words "*Al-Rahmân - Al-Rahîm*".

The attribute *Rahîmiyyat* is mentioned in several passages of the Holy Qur'ân as, for example, it is stated in the Holy Qur'ân: Allâh is *Rahîm* towards the believers; meaning that the disbelievers and the rebellious have no part in it.

It is noteworthy how God has here reserved the operation of the attribute *Rahîmiyyat* for the believers but He has not anywhere indicated that He has reserved *Rahmâniyyat* for them. It is nowhere stated that He is *Rahmân* for the believers. In fact the compassion that is especially reserved for the believers has been called *Rahîmiyyat* every time.

In the Holy Qur'ân we are told: The *Rahîmiyyat* (mercy) of Allâh is very close to those who do good deeds. [66]

وَلَا تُفْسِدُوا فِي الْأَرْضِ بَعْدَ إِصْلَاحِهَا وَادْعُوهُ خَوْفًا وَطَمَعًا ۚ إِنَّ رَحْمَتَ اللَّـهِ
قَرِيبٌ مِنَ الْمُحْسِنِينَ (٥٦)

*And do not create disorder in the land after the fair ordering thereof and call on Him with fear (of His displeasure) and with hope (of His mercy). Surely the mercy of Allâh is always close to the doers of good to others. (7:56)*

Again, in the Holy Qur'ân it is stated: Towards those who believed and left their homes and discarded their personal desires for the sake of Allâh and strove in the cause of Allâh, for Allâh's mercy, Allâh is Most Forgiving, and *Al-Rahim* (ever Merciful). [67]

إِنَّ الَّذِينَ آمَنُوا وَالَّذِينَ هَاجَرُوا وَجَاهَدُوا فِي سَبِيلِ اللَّـهِ أُولَـٰئِكَ يَرْجُونَ رَحْمَتَ
اللَّـهِ ۚ وَاللَّـهُ غَفُورٌ رَحِيمٌ (٢١٨)

[66] *The Holy Qur'ân: explained by 'Allamah Nooruddîn, rendered into English by Mrs. A. R. 'Omar; 'Abdul Mannân 'Omar*
[67] *ibid*

*Verily, as to those who believe and those who emigrate and struggle hard in the cause of Allâh, it is they who do (rightly) hope for Allâh's mercy. And Allâh is Great Protector, Ever Merciful. (2:218)*

In other words, His *Rahîmiyyat* attends those who seek it earnestly. There is none who sought it earnestly and did not achieve it.

**The fourth attribute of *Mâlik e-Youmiddîn:*** The fourth category of Divine grace is the most special grace. By virtue of this grace, Allâh has named Himself *Mâlik e-Youmiddîn* in *Surah Al-Al-Fâtihah.*

This aspect of grace does not manifest itself merely in response to effort and exertion. Its manifestation demands a total negation and utter annihilation of the dark and narrow realm of means and that the perfect might of the One and the only God should shine forth directly in its full splendor without the intermediary of any instrument.

For, in respect of this **ultimate grace** the only addition and perfection that human wisdom can conceive of is that it should be manifested with the utmost clarity, excluding every possible doubt, reservation or imperfection, so that there should be no question concerning its deliberate bestowal on the part of the Gracious Bestower, nor concerning the reality and fullness of the grace, as a mercy.

The munificence and requital of the Eternal Master should become manifest like the brightness of day. At the same time the recipient of grace should feel and realize with the highest degree of certitude that it is indeed the Sovereign of the universe Who has bestowed on him, by His will and command and special power, a mighty favor and a great delight and that in truth he is the recipient of full and lasting reward for his good deeds which is pure and superb, a prized and highly desired boon, and not any kind of test or trial. The manifestation of such perfect, superb and enduring grace should be clear and revealing as to bear Divine attestation that it is free from even a suspicion of trial or test.

This manifestation of grace should further comprehend the highest and most refined pleasures. The pure and perfect quality of which should so completely absorb the heart and soul as should be beyond the power of reason, imagination or fancy to exceed.

This earthly world which is imperfect, illusory, and has limited capacity, thus is not suited to serve as a sphere for those grand manifestations, brilliant lights and eternal bounties, nor can it comprehend those full, perfect and enduring auroras. An altogether different realm is needed for the manifestation of this **perfect, superb and enduring grace**, totally independent of and free from the opaqueness of physical means, adequate to demonstrate the absolute and pure might of the Overpowering Unique Lord – The All mighty God Allâh.

Yet a foretaste of this most special grace is vouchsafed in this very life to those perfect and purified persons who tread wholeheartedly along the path of righteousness and discarding all personal desires and inclinations and devote themselves utterly to One God. For these, in truth, die before death overtakes them and though they subsist in this world they have their being in the hereafter.

Thus, as they wean their minds away from all temporalities and make a break with human ways and values and, turning their faces away from everything beside Allâh, adopt a transcendent mode, the Beneficent Lord also treats them in like manner and manifests His light to them in a manner in which it is not manifested to others except after death, and thus they become recipients in this very life of a portion of the light of this most special grace.

This perfect, superb and enduring grace is the most exclusive of all graces and is the culmination of them. Its recipient attains to the apex of beatitude and ever-lasting felicity which is the fountain head of all joys, and he who is debarred from this grace is condemned to long lasting hell.

By virtue of this most exclusive grace, Allâh has named Himself *Mâlik e-Youmiddîn* (Supreme Master of the Day of Requital) in this *Surah Al-Fâtihah.* The Judgment referred to here is the perfect requital defined in the Honored Qur'ân. That perfect requital, however, demands a perfect manifestation of full Divine Sovereignty which excludes all instrumentality. [68]

يَوْمَ هُمْ بَارِزُونَ ۖ لَا يَخْفَىٰ عَلَى اللَّهِ مِنْهُمْ شَيْءٌ ۚ لِمَنِ الْمُلْكُ الْيَوْمَ ۖ لِلَّهِ الْوَاحِدِ الْقَهَّارِ (١٦)

*The day when they will (all) appear (in their true light) and nothing about them is ever hidden from Allâh. (On that Day they will be asked,) `To whom belongs the sovereignty this day?' They will reply, `(It belongs) only to Allâh, the One, the All-Dominant.' (40:16)*

This means that on that day the Divine attribute of Providence will manifest itself independently of the normal media and it will be seen and felt that nothing counts except the overpowering dominion and perfect sovereignty of the Exalted God Allâh.

[68] *The Holy Qur'ân: explained by 'Allamah Nooruddîn, rendered into English by Mrs. A. R. 'Omar; 'Abdul Mannân 'Omar*

All comfort and joy and requital and reward seen as emanating directly from Allâh, with no screen or barrier in between, nor will there be left any room for any doubt.

Those who had withdrawn themselves from the world for the pleasure and love of Allâh, will find a perfect state of felicity enveloping their bodies and souls and their exterior and interior leaving no part of them outside the embrace of this great happiness.

The phrase *Mâlik e-Youmiddîn* (Supreme Master of the Day of Requital) also connotes that on that day every comfort and torment and pleasure and pain that humans will experience shall proceed directly from Allâh. He will be in truth and in fact the sole Lord of Dispensation; that is to say nearness to Him or distance from Him will determine eternal happiness or everlasting misfortune.

In the sense that on those who had believed in Him and had held fast to Divine Unity and had filled their hearts with His pure love, the light of the mercy of Allâh will descend clearly and manifestly, and those who did not have faith and did not experience Divine love, will be denied this joy and comfort and shall be in painful agony and torment.

**The order of priorities in the 'Book of Nature' are reflected in the 'Book of Revelation':** It is now clear that the attribute *Al-Rahmân* must take precedence over the attribute *Al-Rahîm*; this also satisfies the requirements of proper syntax. For, a glance at the Book of Nature first encounters the *Rabbûbiyat (*universal Providence of Allâh), next His *Rahmâniyyat* (Graciousness and Beneficence) and then His *Rahîmiyyat* (Compassion, Redemption and Mercy) and finally His attribute *Mâlik e-Youmiddîn* (the Supreme Master and sole Dispenser of ultimate reward and punishment).

And elegance of syntax requires that the order of priorities in the Book of Nature should be reflected in the Book of Revelation. Reversal of the natural order in narrative is tantamount to reversal of the law of nature and the natural order. It is an essential requirement that the order of narrative should be in accord with the order of nature so as to reflect it accurately and that whatever has natural and factual priority should have precedence in description also.

The verses under consideration conform to the highest standards of syntax and narrative. It is also a true picture of the natural order as it appears to every beholder.

Is it not the most straightforward approach that Divine bounties should be set out in the Book of Revelation in the same order in which they occur in the Book of Nature? To find fault with such an appropriate and wise order is to confess a lack both of sight and of insight.

The four principal Divine attributes have been therein mentioned in proper order. These Divine attributes are the basic attributes and as the *Surah Fâtihah* itself has been called Mother of the Book these four attributes are Mothers of all attributes.

It's unique and beautifully ordered eloquence which encompasses fine points, rare pearls of wisdom and uncommon insights into Divine purposes. You will not find its parallel among the ancients or among contemporaries. Its literary merits are doubtless of singular excellence and its foothold is far above the mountain-tops of science and it enchants the hearts of the discerning. Now that you have learnt the order of arrangement of these four oceans of Allâh's attributes, you should appreciate it and be of the grateful to Allâh.

# Verse 5

إِيَّاكَ نَعْبُدُ وَإِيَّاكَ نَسْتَعِينُ (٥)

*You alone do we worship, and You alone do we implore for help.*

### Important Arabic Words Used in This Verse

***Iyyâka* اياک*; Na'budu* نعبد*; Nast'aîn* نستعين**

***Iyyaka*** اياک*:(Root Word Iî* ای *and Ka* ک*)*

**Meanings *Iî* ای :** Verily; Yes; Of course; Used in affirming by oath; You Alone; [69]
**Meanings Ka ک:** Thee; You; This particle may be translated according to the content such as: Like that; So; Similarly; Likewise; Even so; So shall it be; So the fact is; [70]

***Na'budu*** نعبد*: (Root Word 'Abada* عبد *)*

**Meanings:** Worship; Obedience combined with complete humility; Submit; Devote; Adore; Accept

[69] *Dictionary of the Holy Qur'ân by 'Abdul Mannân 'Omar (page 38)*
[70] *Dictionary of the Holy Qur'ân by 'Abdul Mannân 'Omar (page 475)*

the impression of a thing; Venerate (to solicit the goodwill); Slave; Serve; Obeisance (expressing deep respect or deferential courtesy) [71] [72]

***Nast'aîn* نستعين *: (Root Word* عان*)***

Meaning: Seek Aid; Implore for Help; Turn and Call for Assistance; Of Middle Age. [73]

[71] *Mufradât fi Gharâib al-Qur'ân by Al-Raghib*
[72] *Dictionary of the Holy Qur'ân by 'Abdul Mannân 'Omar (page 355)*
[73] *Dictionary of the Holy Qur'ân by 'Abdul Mannân 'Omar (p. 395)*

# Pearls of Wisdom

***'Ibâdat*** of Allâh means whole hearted obedience *(<u>T</u>a'at)* combined with complete humility (*<u>Kh</u>u<u>dz</u>û'*), and through seeking and beseaching help *(Isti'ânat)* from Allâh, so as to be successful in this life and the hereafter.

The idea of *'Ibâdat* in Islam is more than a mere verbal declaration of the glory of Allâh. Moreover, it does not merely mean the performance of certain ritual acts of worship e.g. Prayer, Fasting etc... It has a much wider and comprehensive significance.

The Holy Prophet ﷺ is reported to have said, that each and every act performed in obedience to Allâh's command and to seek His good pleasure is an act of *'Ibâdat.*

The Holy Prophet ﷺ said, If you put a morsel of food in the mouth of your wife (with the intention that you are thereby obeying a command and directive of Allâh), you will find the reward there off with Allâh. *'Ibâdat* is being completely absorbed in the love of Allâh and 'take on the impress' of His Hues and Attributes. [74]

صِبْغَةَ اللَّـهِ ۖ وَمَنْ أَحْسَنُ مِنَ اللَّـهِ صِبْغَةً ۖ وَنَحْنُ لَهُ عَابِدُونَ (١٣٨)

*(Assume) the hues and attributes of Allâh! and who is fairer than Allâh in hues and attributes? We are His worshippers ever. "... (2:138)*

[74] *The Holy Qur'ân: explained by 'Allamah Nooruddîn, rendered into English by Mrs. A. R. 'Omar; 'Abdul Mannân 'Omar*

**In this verse the word Na'budu has been mentioned before the word Nast'înu:** The idea of invoking Allâh's help comes after the impulse and action taken to worship. As such a person should first make up his/her mind and take steps to worship Allâh, and only then seek His help for carrying out this resolve. Yes, we should not quit 'beseeching His help during the entire process of the *'Ibâdat* till one reaches the goal.

The use of plural in *Na'budu* and *Nast'înu* directs our attention to a very important point: a person is not alone in this world but is a part and parcel of the society. He should, therefore, seek not to go alone but to carry others also with him on the path of Allâh.

As long as a person does not reform his environment, his own reform cannot make him immune from danger.

Thus, the use of the plural number points to a principle which is of vital importance for the moral, cultural, and spiritual uplift of Muslims.

This principle, of the importance of all members of the society, is also applied in the next verse.

O God of perfect attributes and source of the four graces, we worship Thee alone and in the due performance of duty of worship and in other calls and needs we seek only Thy help. Thou art our only God and in order to reach Thee we choose no other deity as our medium, neither a human nor idol, nor do we rely on our wisdom or our knowledge; in everything we implore Thee, the Absolute Almighty, for help.

"On realizing in our souls Allah's love and care, His grace and mercy, and His power and justice (as Ruler of the Day of judgment). the immediate result is that we bend in the act of worship, and see both our shortcomings and His all-sufficient power. The emphatic form means that not only do we reach the position of worshipping Allah and asking for His help, but we worship. Him alone and ask for His aid only. For there is none other than He worthy of our devotion and able to help us. Then plural "we" indicates that we associate ourselves with all who seek Allah, thus strengthening ourselves and strengthening them in a fellowship of faith". [75]

**Employ your faculties and God given abilities before supplications:** In the juxtaposition: 'You alone do we worship and You alone do we implore for help'; We worship You alone; takes precedence over: We implore Your help; for, a person approaches God in prayer, after having involved and utilized all his faculties in the subject matter of the prayer. It would be impertinent and insolent on his part to come to Allah without using his faculties which are already endowed by God, and without observing the requirements of the Law of Allâh – the Law of nature.

For instance, if a cultivator were to pray to God to bless his field with a plentiful harvest without preparing it and sowing any seed in it, he would be guilty of insolence and mockery. This is what has been called testing and trying God and that is forbidden.

Deeply ponder it and reflect well. It is true that one who does not use his faculties and available means and rushes into prayer does not pray in real, he in fact tries God. It is therefore, necessary to employ all one's faculties before

[75] *The Meaning of the Holy Qur'ân by 'Abdullah Yûsuf 'Alî, Tenth Edition (page 14)*

submitting one's petition and this is the real significance of this prayer.

**Through prayer Allâh creates some factor which becomes the means of the desired improvement and success:** It is necessary that one should first take stock of one's beliefs and effort. It is the way of God to bring about a desired change through change in the means. He creates some factors and circumstances which becomes the means of the desired improvement and success.

Those who consider that if prayer is available, then means become irrelevant should ponder this seriously. They should realize that prayer is in itself a means which activates other means. The precedence of: 'We worship You alone'; over: 'We implore only Your help'; which is a supplication, emphasizes this very important point.

These verses urge towards grateful appreciation of gifts that have been granted already. And that the worshipper may also urge towards non-reliance on one's own competence and ability. Persisting in supplication and prayer in humility with glorification and praise, in a state between fear and hope, like a suckling infant in the arms of the mother, oblivious and uninterested towards the rest of creation and everything on earth.

**We are weak and cannot carry out the duties of Worship without Allâh's help:** These verses also urge towards confession and acknowledgement that we are weak and cannot carry out the duties of Thy worship without Thy help. They urge also towards discarding pride and arrogance and towards holding fast to the power and might of Allâh when affairs become complicated and hardships pile up.

Let not a youth take pride in his vigor, nor an old person rely on his staff, nor a wise one feel elated with his intelligence nor a scholar trust in the accuracy of his knowledge, or the soundness of his understanding or the keenness of his intellect, nor the fervor of his prayers. Allâh does what He pleases, rejects whom He pleases and admits among His chosen ones whom He pleases – based on His Divine Wisdom and Power.

Allâh here teaches His servants a prayer which is a source of happiness for them and says, in effect: O My servants, beg of Me with humility and in lowliness of spirit: Our Lord, we worship Thee alone, but we have to struggle hard and have to grapple with affectation and remorse and distractions and satanic insinuations and confusing ideas and superstitions and dark thoughts. We follow only conjecture and we are not firmly anchored in faith. In this situation we seek only Thy help. We beg Thee for the gift of keenness, eagerness and readiness of heart and overflowing faith and spiritual response and joy and light and for embellishing our hearts with the decor of truth and the garments of delight, so that, by Thy grace, we may achieve our highest goals and arrive at the ocean of Reality.

In the phrase: **We worship Thee alone;** Allâh, the Supreme, urges His servants to put forth, in their obedience to Him, the utmost energetic effort, standing upright, constantly responding to His call, with: Lord, we spare no pains in our striving and in observing Thy commands and in seeking Thy pleasure; but we seek Thy help and Thy protection against pride and self-esteem and beg of Thee to grant us the strength that would lead us to Thy guidance and to winning Thy pleasure. We are firm in our obedience to Thee and in Thy worship; so write us down among those who submit to Thee.

**We should prove, in a practical manner, that we believe Allâh to be our God in truth:** There is yet another point to be noted in this context. The worshipper declares: Lord, we have adopted Thee alone for worship, preferring Thee over all else and we adore nothing save Thy countenance and we believe in Thy Unity.

It is important that a worshipper should not stop at mere profession that he believes Allâh to be the possessor of His four principal attributes. He should prove, in a practical manner, that He believes Allâh to be His Lord in truth, affirming His Providence *(Rabbûbiyyat)* through his personal practice. One who does not believe in God as his Deity will act as it pleases him; he may commit evil like theft or adultery. But he who professes belief, until he proves his profession by conduct is not entitled to be called a believer, nor can he win grace as the favorites and righteous of the past won it. Faith is itself a grace of God. When it arrives the believer no longer practices vice. Mere words do not work out a person's salvation.

**Verbal affirmations have no meaning unless they are supported by Action and Conduct:** The believer should not merely verbally confess the God, he should so conduct himself as to make it manifest that he truly believes that Allâh alone is His Lord and Provider and not anyone else. Firmly holding that it is Allâh alone Who requites deeds and is aware of the most secret and closely hidden sins and defaults.

Remember, verbal affirmations have no meaning unless they are supported by conduct. One who truly believes Allah to be his Provider and Master of the Day of Requital, can never be guilty of theft, gambling, vice and other misdeeds, for, he knows that all these are fatal poisons and indulgence in them is open disobedience of Divine commands.

In short, until a person demonstrates by conduct that he has firm and true faith in God, he cannot hope for the graces and bounties that are bestowed on the favored ones of God.

Go through the Holy Qur'ân. You will not find anything in it to show that Allah is pleased with those who disregard and ignore the ways that lead to His pleasure. He is pleased only when one follows the ways that Allah himself has appointed for the purpose.

**Allâh urges the Muslims towards mutual accord, unity, and love:** In this verse Allâh, the Lord of Glory and Majesty, has instructed the use of the first person plural, conveying thereby that this prayer is for the benefit of all fellow humans and not only for the benefit of the supplicant.

Thus Allâh urges the members of the society towards mutual accord, unity and love and requires that a supplicant should put himself to hardship for the promotion of his brother/sister's welfare as he would put himself to hardship for the promotion of his own well-being, and should be his brother/sister's well-wisher with all his heart.

Give one another gifts of prayer as brothers/sisters and friends exchange gifts, and widen the scope of your prayers and your motives and your aims, making room in them for your brethren and become like brothers, sisters, fathers and sons in mutual affection.

**Worshipper should be completely absorbed in the love of Allâh:** The essence of worship is that the worshipper should feel as if he is in the presence of Allâh, or at least that God sees him. He should be free completely from every diverting and distracting tendency, and keep in view only Allâh's greatness and His Providence.

He should continue addressing to Allâh in prayers and have repeated recourse to *tauba* (seeking refuge with Allâh) and *Istighfar* (seeking forgiveness and avoidance of wrongs and evolving to higher stages of salvation).

A worshiper should repeatedly confess his own helplessness, so that his self may be purified and his communion with Allah may be strengthened and he should be completely absorbed in His love.

**Does worship only comprise many prostrations, repeated obeisance and standing at attention position?** People boast of worshipping God. But does worship only comprise many prostrations, repeated obeisance and standing at attention or do those who tell their beads over and over deserve to be called worshippers of Allah? Indeed not!

Only he is capable of worship whom the love of Allah draws so close that his own self is excluded altogether. First, there should be full faith in the Existence of Allah and then full knowledge of His Beauty and Beneficence and then there should be the attachment of love with Him, constantly aflame in the bosom, radiating itself at all times in the face.

The impression of His magnificence on the heart should be so deep that the entire world should appear like dead in contrast with Him; every fear should derive from Him alone and all pleasure should be in His love and all joy in seclusion with Him and no comfort without Him. If and when one's condition is such this is the state of true worship.

But this state cannot be achieved without the special help of God. Therefore, the Supreme Being taught the prayer: We worship Thee alone and implore Thee alone for help; that is, we cannot carry out worship in the true sense unless there is special help forthcoming from Thee.

Worshipping Allâh as the real object of all love is true saintliness, beyond which there is no higher degree, but this is unattainable except with His help. It is attained when His magnificence is imprinted on the heart and the heart is filled with His love and relies totally on Him and chooses Him alone and prefers Him to all else, making His remembrance its only goal. This is a very narrow door and a very bitter draught. Few enter this door and few quaff this draught.

God made human and sent down for him a law and prescribed rules and penalties. The primary object of all this is not that he should attain to salvation. Human has been created for perpetual servitude of God. The object of his religious life is eternal serfdom of God; salvation being its necessary concomitant, attainment to which results from the achievement of the true objective. Freedom from sin is also not the object of law and the ordinances. For freedom from sin is also a concomitant of the true objective.

**Salvation through sincerity and steadfastness:** When human takes to worship and obedience he is necessarily freed from sin, being far removed from it. When he is freed from sin he is saved from the consequences of sin. The way to salvation, therefore, is to stand in an attitude of sincerity and steadfastness before the Source of all light whence rays of light descend.

That posture has been called *Istiqâmat* (uprightness) as Allâh, the Sublime, says: Stand upright as thou hast been commanded. [76]

فَاسْتَقِمْ كَمَا أُمِرْتَ وَمَن تَابَ مَعَكَ وَلَا تَطْغَوْا ۚ إِنَّهُ بِمَا تَعْمَلُونَ بَصِيرٌ (١١٢)

*So stand you upright, as you have been commanded, and (also) those who (have left their evil ways and) turned to Allâh (in repentance) and joined you. Do not exceed the bounds (set by Allâh, O people!). He indeed is Observer of your deeds (11:112)*

**Rays of light will descend on whoso stands before the Source of light:** There is no doubt that rays of light will descend on whoso stands before the Source of light and through the descent of light will be dispelled that darkness which is called sinfulness. We know that no darkness is dispelled without the descent of light. God, the Supreme, sends light to dispel darkness. Darkness cannot stay before light.

It may be asked when a person be said to have taken his stand before the Source of all light. The answer is that this would be said when he turns over to righteousness in all aspects of his life and loves truth and sin is no longer attractive to him, in fact he looks upon it with abhorrence and seeks the help of God to deliver him from it. God, the Gracious, the Compassionate then helps him and sends down His light to deliver him from this darkness.

This prayer is taught for this very purpose indeed: We seek Thy help in this affliction. Help us take our stand in the path of the descent of the rays of Thy grace.

---

[76] *The Holy Qur'ân: explained by 'Allamah Nooruddîn, rendered into English by Mrs. A. R. 'Omar; 'Abdul Mannân 'Omar*

**Essence of worship is to take on the attributes and complexion of the worshipped:** The words of Allâh, the Exalted: 'Thee alone do we worship and Thee alone do we implore for help'; indicate that all good fortune is comprised in putting oneself in accord with the attributes of the Lord of the worlds. The essence of worship is to take on the complexion of the worshipped One and that is in the eyes of the righteous the culmination of beatitude.

A worshipper is not a worshipper in truth, unless his character reflects the attributes of Allâh. Therefore, one feature of true worship is that a providence reflecting the ***Rabbûbiyat*** (Providence) of the Lord of Honor, should take its birth in the worshipper and in a similar way the attributes of ***Rahmâni****yyat* (Graciousness), ***Rahîmi****yyat* (Mercy and Compassion) and ***Mâlikiyyat e-Youmiddîn*** (Mastership of judgment and Requital) should be reflected in him. This is the right path which we have been commanded to seek and this is the way that we have been urged to hope for from Allâh - the Bounteous Lord of immense grace.

**Vanity and arrogance eat up all virtuous acts:** Since the principal obstructions in the way of the attainment of these degrees are vanity, which eats up all virtuous acts, and arrogance which is the root of all evils.

Allâh has in His mercy for the weak who are prone to error and by way of compassion for those seeking Him, indicated the remedies for these 'maladies. He has directed that we should say: 'We worship Thee'; so that we may be delivered of vanity, and has directed that we should say: 'We implore Thy help'; so that we may be cured of arrogance and boastfulness.

His direction: We worship Thee; is an incentive towards cultivation of sincerity and complete submission and His direction: We implore Thy help; is a supplication for strength, firmness and uprightness, and His direction.

**Five daily prayers are the highest form of worship:** The highest worship is constant watchfulness over the five daily Prayer services (*Salat*) in the early portion of their timing and to endeavor with eager attention to derive the utmost blessing there from, through strict observance of obligatory and voluntary parts.

For, formal Prayer (*Salat*) is a mount that carries the worshipper to the Almighty God Allâh, transporting him to a station he could not reach on the back of fast-running horses or fast moving modes of transportation. The object of Prayer cannot be achieved with arrows and through the barrel of guns, and its mystery cannot be unfolded by pens and worldly intellect alone.

Whoso makes this method of the five daily Prayer services (*Salat*) obligatory on himself arrives at the truth and discovers the reality and meets the Friend Who is hidden behind the screens of invisibility, and is delivered from doubt and uncertainty. His days become bright, his words shine like pearls, his face becomes refulgent like the full moon and his station is elevated.

Whoso makes himself lowly before Allâh in Prayer *(Salat)* will find that God makes kings humble before him and makes such a slave a master.

**You should love your enemy as you love yourself and your children:** This verse also conveys that it is not possible for a person to worship truly without the grant of strength from the Presence of the One, the only God. One of the elements of worship is that you should love your enemy as you love yourself and your children, and that you should overlook the faults of others and forbear.

Be good-hearted and pure-minded, upright and clean-living and loyal and virtuous, free from evil inclinations; and that you should be of service to humanity with a natural inclination, without formality and without affectation; and that you should not hurt your less fortunate brother with your arrogance, nor injure him with harsh words.

It is obligatory on you to respond to your aggrieved brother with courtesy and never speak to him contemptuously. You should die before your death and count yourself among the dead. Honor your visitor even if he be dressed in tattered rags and not in gorgeous robes and new garments. Greet with the salutation of peace, both the acquaintance and the stranger and be ever ready to share the burdens of others.

**Employ God-given talents and faculties and only then to appeal for Divine help for its fruition:** It is necessary to employ one's God-given talents and faculties in promoting a temporal or spiritual undertaking before seeking Divine help and then to appeal for Divine help for its fruition. God has taught us this in our daily prayer. He has commanded us to pray: We serve and worship Thee and seek Thy help; and not: We seek Thy help and serve and worship Thee!

One who seeks through prayer and effort is a righteous person. The one who does not seek with full understanding and intelligence and power, is not a seeker in the sight of Allâh, and a person who tries Allâh in this manner is ever frustrated. But if, along with his effort, he also supplicates Allâh then Allâh saves him, even if he should make a slip.

But Allâh cares not for one who comes to His door in self-assurance and sloth and thus tests God.

There is no greater boon for a man than that he should hate sin, and that God, the Supreme, may be pleased to safeguard him against disobedience. But this cannot be attained merely through effort or merely by prayer but through both jointly; as God, the Exalted, has taught: 'We worship Thee alone and we implore Thy help'. This means that one employs one's God-granted powers and capacities in the best manner and commits the result to God with the supplication addressed to the Supreme Lord.

One who does not make use of his God-granted powers and faculties but seeks help merely through prayer is in error. How can he ever succeed in his objective? The true believer makes use of both effort and prayer. He plans well and puts forth his best effort and then leaving the matter in the hands of the All Mighty God - Allâh.

**Honest Effort and sincere prayer should be combined:** The righteous who have been promised great success in the Holy Qur'ân are those who mind their obligations to the fullest, keeping steadfast in righteousness as far as their human capacities permit, until they arrive at the limit of their capacities and then they beg God for further strength, as is evident from the prayer: 'We worship Thee and seek Thy help'. We worship Thee; means we have done what we could to the limit of our capacities sparing no pains; now: We implore Thy help; meaning we continue to seek new strength from Thee.

This conveys that in every righteous undertaking, one should make use of one's powers and capacities and should plan and work hard. One who devotes himself solely to prayer but does not make any effort, does not gain his purpose. If a cultivator having done the sowing of the seed puts forth no further effort, how can he expect a good harvest? This is the way of Allâh.

Those who depend on their own resources and disregard God, the Sublime, never come to a good and fruitful end. This does not mean that not doing anything and sitting idle is reliance on God. Using one's resources and God-given capacities is appreciation of God's bounties.

Those who do not make use of their capacities and proclaim their trust in Allah are mistaken and confused. They do not truly appreciate Allâh, the Sublime. They try the Supreme Lord and in effect treat their God-given powers and faculties as superfluous and irrelevant and are thus guilty of irreverence and impertinence towards Him. They ignore the significance of: 'We worship Thee'; and without practicing it, seek to enjoy the benefits of: 'We implore Thy help'. This is most improper.

One must make use of one's resources, as far as possible, within the limits of one's capacities, without relying on them as one's deities and sources of beneficence. Instead, having made proper use of them, one must submit the matter to Allâh, with a thanksgiving prostration for the Divine gift of faculties and capacities.

**Thanksgiving prostration to Allâh for the Divine gift of faculties, capacities and life itself:** *Iyyaka na'budu* إِيَّاكَ نَعْبُدُ means: We adore Thee, making use of all the resources and means that Thou hast granted us. If this tongue in our mouth, which is made up of veins and muscles had not been what it is we would not have been able to speak. He granted us a tongue that can express the thoughts of the mind. There are many ailments which could suspend all activity of the tongue, were any of them to afflict it, making one dumb. How wonderful then is this gift of the tongue! If we do not employ the tongue for prayer, it would be our misfortune.

Similarly if the structure of the ears were prejudicially affected, one could become stone deaf. The same is true of the mind and intellect. Humility, lowliness, the faculty of thought and reflection would all be stultified in case of distemper or disorder. Do we not observe how the mental faculties disintegrate in the case of the insane? Is it not then incumbent upon us to appreciate these God-given gifts?

If we let these faculties that Allâh, the Exalted, has granted us by His perfect grace, rust by disuse we would undoubtedly be guilty of ingratitude. Be mindful, therefore, that if you pray, leaving your talents and capacities unexercised, the prayer is of no avail. For, if the primary bounties are not utilized, how can one be expected to use and to derive benefit from further bounties? We worship Thee; is a confession: O Lord of universal providence, we have not neglected Thy first gift.

**To be able to tread the straight path one must use faculties appropriately and supplicate:** Thus, unless one makes full use of the Divine grace that has been extended to one through *Ra<u>h</u>mâniyyat* and then makes one's prayer, one cannot hope for any good result. The law of nature demands that we should make good use of that which has already been bestowed upon us and then supplicate for more.

When a person says: 'We worship Thee and implore Thy help'; and sets out with sincerity and loyalty, then God, the Sublime, causes to spring forth a wide stream of righteousness which flows down on his heart filling it with the spirit of righteousness. A person approaches with a paltry offering, but Allâh, the Exalted, bestows on him a precious gift of immense value. He is then granted a volume of insights and verities and strength of immense value.

**The essence of the struggle to attain to the excellence of *Saddîq* (The Righteous) lies in a person's submission to Allâh:** The essence of the struggle to attain to the excellence of *Saddîq* (The Righteous) lies in a person's submission: 'We worship Thee'. To the extent of his capacity and potential, in full realization of his feebleness and nothingness, he determines to adhere to truthfulness and to discard falsehood. He turns away from every type of uncleanness and foulness that is inherent in falsehood, and keeps to his firm resolve never to tell a lie or to bear false witness or ever to utter anything false in a fit of temper or in idle talk, or for seeking a benefit, or to ward off harm, or under any circumstances whatever. By binding himself down so far he goes a certain distance in carrying out: We worship Thee. That in itself is worship of high quality. 'We worship Thee'; is followed by: 'We implore Thy help'. Whether he utters these words or not, Allâh, the Sublime, the Source of all grace, and of truth and righteousness, necessarily helps him and reveals to him the high tenets and verities of righteousness.

In: 'We worship Thee'; one is moved by the beauty and beneficence of the Lord of Universal Providence *(Rabb),* the Gracious *(Rahmân),* the Compassionate and Merciful *(Rahîm)* and the Master of the Day of Requital *(Mâlik e-Youmiddîn);* and simultaneously one's humility and the consciousness of one's utter helplessness impel one to cry out: 'We implore Thy help' . Who can be more righteous than one who carries out the duties of worship and supplicates for Divine help in carrying them out.

**In the initial stages of spiritual effort there is often a feeling of constriction, but...:** Some people complain that they do not find comfort in Prayer. They should go back to it repeatedly. In the initial stages of spiritual effort there is often a feeling of constriction. At such time one should repeatedly supplicate: We worship Thee and we implore Thy help.

But to submit this prayer and acquire this strength one needs sincerity and a consuming urge and this is attainable by conjuring up the picture of the robber who is close at the heels and seeks to expose one's nakedness, as he did with Adam. Once this comes to the mind, the soul will cry out: 'We worship Thee and we implore Thy help'.

Satan approaches in the character of a thief and a burglar. One should supplicate the Lord against him, seeking to be safeguarded against the depredations of the robber by Divine support. Those who occupy themselves with this entreaty and are not wearied receive a new power and a new strength where with Satan is vanquished.

One should constantly keep to the prayer: We worship Thee alone and implore only Thy help; and seek strength from Him only. By means of this a person can become a manifestation of Divine glory.

When the moon faces the sun, it receives light from the sun, but when it starts moving away it grows darker and darker. The same is true of a human. So long as he is prostrate at His portal, believing himself to be utterly dependent on Him, Allâh, the Sublime, raises him up and bestows His grace on Him. When he begins to rely on his own strength he is humiliated.

One must proceed to the point of perfection in purity, empty out the heart of everything other than Allâh, and lose one's separate identity. This unity is achieved in its perfection only when one is so utterly possessed by passion for the Divine that it extinguishes the ego completely.

This is not attainable through knowledge, or effort but only through Divine grace. That is why the dedicated worshippers have the cry: We implore Thy help; constantly on their lips. Those who rely on their own strength and do not depend on Allâh are humiliated

The phrase: 'We worship Thee alone'; repudiates all false gods and furnishes a refutation of the polytheists. First the perfect attributes of God, the Supreme, are mentioned and then He is addressed: 'Thee alone do we worship'. That is to say: O Lord of perfect attributes, Lord of universal Providence, Grace, Mercy, Master of the Day of Requital, we worship Thee alone, and we implore of Thy help.

# Verses 6

اهْدِنَا الصِّرَاطَ الْمُسْتَقِيمَ (٦)

*Lead us on the exact right path till we reach the goal,*

### Important Arabic Wordes Used In This Verse

***Ahdina*** اهدنا; ***Al- Sirât*** الصراط; ***Al-Mustaqîm*** المستقيم

***Ahdina*** **اهدنا:** (Root Word: *Hada* هدى):

**Meanings:** Guide; Show with kindness the right path;Lead to the right path; Make one follow the right path till one reaches the goal. [77]

*Al- Sirât* الصراط : (Root Word: *Sirât* صراط)

Meaning: A path which is even, wide enough and can be trodden without difficulty; Way that is straight so that all

[77] *Dictionary of the Holy Qur'ân by 'Abdul Mannân 'Omar (page 588-589)*

part of it are in orderly array and are properly adjusted to one another. [78] [79]

The Arab Lexicologists do not regard a **PATH** as *Sirât* until it comprises the following five prominent features:
i. Being the shortest
ii. Being broad in width for travellers
iii. Leading surely to the objective
iv. Rectitude (leading to rightness of principle or conduct)
v. As the road to the goal in the eyes of the wayfarers [80]

***Al-Mustaqîm* المستقيم :** (Root Word: *Qâma* قام)

**Meanings:** Straight; Right; Undeviating; Without any crookedness; Right Direction; Keep a thing or an affair in a right state; Stand up Errect; Stand still; Stand firm; Rise; ... [81] [82] [83]

[78] *Dictionary of the Holy Qur'ân by 'Abdul Mannân 'Omar (page 313)*
[79] *Mufradât fi Gharâib al-Qur'ân by Al-Raghib*
[80] *Dictionary of the Holy Qur'ân by 'Abdul Mannân 'Omar (page 313)*
[81] *Dictionary of the Holy Qur'ân by 'Abdul Mannân 'Omar (page 471)*
[82] *Mufradât fi Gharâib al-Qur'ân by Al-Raghib*
[83] *The Arabic English Lexicon, E. W. Lane*

# Pearls of Wisdom

*Ahdina* اهدنا **as used in the Holy Qur'ân:**[84]

وَهَدَيْنَاهُ النَّجْدَيْنِ (١٠)

*And We have pointed out to him the two conspicuous high ways (of right and wrong)? (90:10)*

وَالَّذِينَ جَاهَدُوا فِينَا لَنَهْدِيَنَّهُمْ سُبُلَنَا ۚ وَإِنَّ اللَّـهَ لَمَعَ الْمُحْسِنِينَ (٦٩)

*And those who strive hard in Our cause We will certainly guide them in the ways that lead to Us. Verily, Allâh is always with the doers of good (who strive for excellence). (29:69)*

وَقَالُوا الْحَمْدُ لِلَّـهِ الَّذِي هَدَانَا لِهَٰذَا وَمَا كُنَّا لِنَهْتَدِيَ لَوْلَا أَنْ هَدَانَا اللَّـهُ ... (٤٣)

*... and they shall say, `All perfect and true praise belongs to Allâh Who guided us to attain to this (Paradise). We could never have been led aright (to this) if Allâh had not guided us... (7: 43)*

Allâh has taught this prayer in plural form. Guide **us**, and not Guide **me** to point out that prayer for such blessings should not be self-centered but must include the entire humanity.[85]

شَهْرُ رَمَضَانَ الَّذِي أُنْزِلَ فِيهِ الْقُرْآنُ هُدًى لِلنَّاسِ وَبَيِّنَاتٍ مِنَ الْهُدَىٰ وَالْفُرْقَانِ ... (١٨٥)

*The (lunar) month of Ramadzân is that in which the Qur'ân (started to be) revealed as a guidance for the whole of humankind with its clear evidences (providing*

---

[84] *The Holy Qur'ân: explained by 'Allamah Nooruddîn, rendered into English by Mrs. A. R. 'Omar; 'Abdul Mannân 'Omar*

[85] *ibid*

*comprehensive) guidance and the Discrimination (between right and wrong). (2:185)*

وَأَنِ اعْبُدُونِي ۚ هَٰذَا صِرَاطٌ مُسْتَقِيمٌ (٦١)

*`And (did I not charge you) to worship Me, (for) this is the straight and right path? (36:61)*

This wonderful prayer in this verse is not confined to things spiritual or to things of material nature only, but covers the entire field of human endeavor and requirements - both material and spiritual.[86]

The prayer embodied in this verse requires us not to be satisfied with 'being shown a path', or even with being 'led up to it', but ever to go on following it 'till we reach the goal/destination'.

Surah *Al-Fâtihah* comprises so many verities and such treasures of wisdom and insight that it would take volumes to set them out at length. Consider this one prayer so pregnant with wisdom that has been taught in this Surah.

It is comprehensive enough to provide the key for the achievement of all temporal and spiritual objectives. We cannot have any idea of the nature of an object nor can we derive any benefit from it until we find the right way of approach to it. The difficult and complex problems of life whether they relate to matters of state or administration or to fighting and war and hostilities, or to theories of natural sciences or astronomy, or to crafts or methods of diagnosis and therapy, or to commerce and agriculture, are hard, even impossible, to resolve, until one finds the correct way of approach to them.

[86] *ibid*

The supplication: 'Guide us along the straight path till we reach the goal'; comprehends all mundane and spiritual requirements; for, until the right way of approach is available in respect of a problem, there can be no progress.

A physician, a farmer, in short everyone needs the right approach and the right way in respect of every undertaking. When a Physician learns the correct method of diagnosing the disease and identifying the right prescription he will have found the right path to practicing the medical profession and will succeed.

Similarly, there is a right approach for everyone, lawyers, professionals, scientists, etc. When the correct approach is discovered the rest becomes easy.

Seek of Allâh all our requirements, major and minor, without hesitation, for He is the true God. One who prays most for the right way and right guidance and then acts accordingly is the most virtuous.

In the verse: Lead us along the straight path till we reach the goal; there is an urge towards praying for true understanding; as if Allâh is teaching us by urging us to call upon Him so that He may demonstrate to us His attributes as they really are and may include us among the grateful.

If we translate by the English word "guide," we shall have to say: "Guide us to and in the straight Way." For we may be wandering aimlessly, and the first step is to find the Way; and the second need is to keep in the Way: Our own wisdom may fail in either case. The straight Way is often the narrow Way, or the steep Way, which many people shun (see 90:11).

By the world's perversity the straight Way is sometimes stigmatized and the crooked Way praised. How are we to judge? We must ask for Allah's guidance. With a little spiritual insight we shall see which are the people who walk in the light of Allah's grace, and which are those that walk in the darkness of wrath. This also would help our judgment. [87]

**The prayer requires a believer not to be satisfied with only being shown a path, or even with being led up to it, but ever to go on following it till he reaches the goal:** This part of the prayer covers material and spiritual needs, present, and future: The believer prays for being shown the straight path-the shortest path. Sometimes a person is shown the right and straight path but is not led up to it, or, if he is led up to it, he fails to stick to it and follow it to the end. The prayer requires a believer not to be satisfied with only being shown a path, or even with being led up to it, but ever to go on following it till he reaches the goal.

This being the significance of *Hiddayah* which means, to show the right path (90:10), to lead to the right path (29:69) and to make one follow the right path (7:43).

In fact, we need God's help at every step and at every moment, and it is imperative that we should ever be offering to God the supplication embodied in the verse. Constant praying, therefore, is necessary. As long as we have requirements unfulfilled and needs unsatisfied and goals unattained, we stand in need of prayer till we reach the ultimate goal and destination of Paradise.

---

[87] *The Meaning of the Holy Qur'ân by 'Abdullah Yûsuf 'Alî, Tenth Edition (page 15)*

**Three stages of human development:** The teaching of the most authentic Book of Allâh and of the Prophet of Allâh (Peace and blessings of Allâh be on him) is divisible into three parts.

**First** that the wild ones should be tamed into human beings and should be taught proper behavior and be equipped with human susceptibilities.

**Secondly**, they may be promoted from average human beings to the highest stage of moral excellence.

**Thirdly,** that they may be raised from the ethical level to the level of the love of the Creator so that they may attain to the stage of closeness to the Divine and His pleasure and His company and immersion in Him and a melting-down in His love and absorption in Him. This is the stage where one's self and choice are shed and Allâh alone remains just as He alone will survive the annihilation of this universe, in His Supremacy. This then is the last stage of the pilgrims' journeying to Allah, men and women, and here terminate all strivings and here end all the paths of saintliness.

This is the final stage of steadfastness that is the object of the *Al-Fâtihah* prayer. All the vain desires generated by the promptings of the evil-bidding ego flare up and are consumed at this stage under the command of the Lord of Might and Honor. And it is asked: Whose is the dominion today? Surely of the Lord of Power.

**Seeking guidance from Allah is like turning to an eminent physician for healing:** The seeking of guidance from God then is like turning to an eminent physician and placing oneself wholly in the hands of the healer. The bounty which Allâh has indicated for His servants is the utter detachment of the worshipper from the world and his turning wholly to Allâh, and Allâh's reciprocating him with His blessings and His inspiration and His responsive favors and dignifying him among His own dignified ones and admitting him among His protected servants, and His direction: [88]

قُلْنَا يَا نَارُ كُونِي بَرْدًا وَسَلَامًا عَلَىٰ إِبْرَاهِيمَ (٦٩)

*We said, `O fire, be you a means of coolness and safety for Abraham. (21:69)*

The word *Sirat* means the way that is straight, so that all parts of it are in orderly array and are properly adjusted to one another.

People gifted with God-Consciousness and God-fearing hearts and gifted with light of knowledge do not regard a way *(Târiq)* as the path *(Sirat)* until it comprises five of the prominent features of the faith and these are

(l) rectitude and righteousness of the objective (2) leading surely to the objective (3) being the shortest (4) and being broad in width for travelers ease and comfort (5) and its determination as the road to the objective in the eyes of the wayfarers.

***Istiqâmat* استقامت (Steadfastness) wins the pleasure of Allâh:** *Istiqâmat* is another derivative word from the same root word for *Mustaqîm.* It is very true that Steadfastness is more than a miracle. The climax of steadfastness is that in front of all-enveloping afflictions, with life and honor and prestige in jeopardy in the cause of Allâh, with no redeeming feature to afford relief. Even

[88] *The Holy Qur'ân: explained by 'Allamah Nooruddîn, rendered into English by Mrs. A. R. 'Omar; 'Abdul Mannân 'Omar*

God, by way of trial, shutting the door to an uplifting vision, dream, or revelation, leaving one exposed to frightful terrors.

One should not lose heart, shrinking back like a coward and should let nothing impair the integrity of loyalty, sincerity and firmness, welcoming humiliation, being reconciled to death, refusing to look to a friend for reinforcement of steadfastness and support, for it is the hour of crisis. In spite of being totally friendless and weak and without anything to hearten one, to stand upright and proffer one's neck, saying: Come what may; without a word of protest, to the determined decree, neither exhibiting desperation nor having recourse to plaintive moaning until the conditions of the trial have been fully satisfied.

This is steadfastness indeed by means of which Allâh is reached. It is the fragrance of this that is exuded by the dust of Prophets and Apostles and the righteous and the martyrs. It is to this that the Lord of glory and majesty has pointed in the prayer: O Allâh show us the path of uprightness, the path that leads to Your favors and gifts and pleases You.

Allâh has pointed to the same in another verse[89]:

وَمَا تَنْقِمُ مِنَّا إِلَّا أَنْ آمَنَّا بِآيَاتِ رَبِّنَا لَمَّا جَاءَتْنَا ۚ رَبَّنَا أَفْرِغْ عَلَيْنَا صَبْرًا وَتَوَفَّنَا مُسْلِمِينَ (١٢٦)

*And you find no fault in us but that we have believed in the signs of our Lord when they came to us (and we pray to Him), "Our Lord! Pour-forth upon us patience and perseverance and grant that we die in a state of complete submission (to You)".' (7:126).*

[89] *Ibid*

During the period of hardships and afflictions, God, the Sublime, sends down a light on the hearts of His chosen favorites who bear all calamities with good cheer. In the ecstasy of faith they kiss the fetters that their feet may have to bear in His way.

In fact, the true lover goes forward at the hour of affliction and,' holding life of no account, lays aside the love of life and places himself entirely at the disposal of His Lord, seeking only His pleasure.

As Allâh, the Sublime, says: [90]

وَمِنَ النَّاسِ مَنْ يَشْرِي نَفْسَهُ ابْتِغَاءَ مَرْضَاتِ اللَّهِ ۗ وَاللَّهُ رَءُوفٌ بِالْعِبَادِ (٢٠٧)

*Of the people there is he who sacrifices his very life seeking the pleasure of Allâh. And Allâh is very Kind and Compassionate toward such (of His) servants. (2:207)*

Such is the spirit of steadfastness that leads to Allah – our God. Let him ponder who will.

*Istiqâmat* (steadfastness) is identical with *fana* (sacrifice of self) the term used by the *Sufis* (saint-scholars). They interpret: Guide us along the straight path; also as meaning *fana*; that is to say, the soul, emotions and designs should all be devoted to Allâh, the Exalted, and all one's personal sentiments and desires should suffer a total death. Those who do not give priority to the will and designs of Allâh, the Supreme, over their personal aims and concerns, depart this life in the midst of the frustration of their mundane affairs and aims.[91]

---

[90] *The Holy Qur'ân: explained by 'Allamah Nooruddîn, rendered into English by Mrs. A. R. 'Omar; 'Abdul Mannân 'Omar*

[91] *Ibid*

Allâh, the Supreme, has drawn attention to it in: 'Guide us along the straight path'; and in another place has said:

إِنَّ الَّذِينَ قَالُوا رَبُّنَا اللَّـهُ ثُمَّ اسْتَقَامُوا تَتَنَزَّلُ عَلَيْهِمُ الْمَلَائِكَةُ أَلَّا تَخَافُوا وَلَا تَحْزَنُوا وَأَبْشِرُوا بِالْجَنَّةِ الَّتِي كُنْتُمْ تُوعَدُونَ (٣٠)

*Verily, those who say, `Allâh is our Lord,' and then remain steadfast (and follow the straight path), the angels will descend upon them (saying), `Have no fear nor grieve rather rejoice at the glad tidings of receiving the Gardens (of Paradise) which you have been promised.*
*(Ch.41:Verse30)*

## The natural order may be described as Mustaqîm:

What does steadfastness *Istiqâmat* mean? When everything is in place and in order, it is appraised as wisdom and *Istiqâmat*. For instance, were the components of a telescope or computer to be dislocated and dispersed out of order, it will not work. Thus, placing a thing in its proper position is *Istiqâmat* steadfastness.

In other words, the 'natural order' may be described as *Mustaqîm*. Unless the human mold is maintained in its natural order and in its normal condition, it cannot develop its excellences.

The proper way of prayer is that the loftiest name of God, Allâh, and the steadfastness of the supplicant, should be combined with the natural order of things, and the supplicant should turn only to Allah and to no one else, not even to the idol of his ambitions and desires. When this state is reached one realizes the significance of: [92]

---

[92] *The Holy Qur'ân: explained by 'Allamah Nooruddîn, rendered into English by Mrs. A. R. 'Omar; 'Abdul Mannân 'Omar*

وَقَالَ رَبُّكُمُ ادْعُونِي أَسْتَجِبْ لَكُمْ ۚ

*And your Lord says, `Call on Me,*
*I will answer your prayer... (40 60)*

These verses are treasures full of meanings. As for the words of the sublime Lord: Guide us and lead us along the straight path; they mean: Show us the straight path, guide us along the way and keep us constant along the course that leads to Thy presence and Mercy and safeguards from Thy punishment.

The way of finding guidance is to be looked and gathered from the Divine Book, The Holy Qur'ân and the *Uswah* (the life example of the Holy Prophet)'. The first is seeking knowledge of the Divine with the help of reason and demonstrable proof; secondly, through self-purification and rigorous self-discipline; and thirdly, through total turning to Allâh, with sincere love and beseeching His help in whole-hearted alignment with His will. And ruling out the least disparity and returning to Him with entreaties and prayers and a firm resolve.

**Putting everything in its proper place is 'straight path':** Observance of true virtue is treading 'the straight path' which is also called following the middle way of moderation. For practical faith, which is the real objective, is attained through it. Whosoever is slack in seeking this degree of righteousness falls short and one who impels himself to go beyond is guilty of excess.

For instance, being clement on every occasion is excess: for it is of the essence of virtue that the propriety of the place and occasion be duly observed. On the other hand, never showing mercy on any occasion is to fall short, for both occasion and place are missed. Putting everything in its proper place is 'moderation', and this is the 'Straight Path'. Thus it is the duty of every Muslim to tread and follow.

The nature of *S̲irat-al-mustaqîm* is 'truth and wisdom'. If truth and wisdom are exercised towards the creatures of God, 'that is virtue'; if they are exercised in respect of God 'that means sincerity and righteousness'; and if they are exercised towards oneself, 'that is purification of self'. *S̲irat-al-mustaqîm* comprises all three, virtue, sincerity of faith, and self-purification.

Thus the Supplication for 'the straight path' has been prescribed for a Muslim in every Prayer service for this would keep him firmly established in the fundamental principle of Divine Unity.

**Sirat-al-Mustaqîm has Three sets of obligations:** It should be understood that *S̲irat-al-mustaqîm* which is based on truth and wisdom has three aspects, theoretical, practical and relating to self. Each of these is again three faceted.

For instance, the **theoretical** comprises appreciation of that which is due and obligation to Allâh, that which is due and obligation to His creatures, and that which is due and obligation to oneself.

The **practica**l life demands the discharge of each of these three sets of obligations.

This is the theory of *S̲irat-al-mustaqîm* concerning 'that which is due and obligation to Allâh'. Its practical aspect comprises obeying Him with perfect sincerity, associating no one in the obedience due to Him, and supplicating Him alone looking up only to Him for the promotion of one's welfare and effacing oneself in His love.

The theoretical *Sirat-al-mustaqîm*, concerning that which is due and obligation to one's fellow human beings, consists in accepting them as one's kin. For, true appraisal of God's creatures is that their existence is only derived from Him and is non-existent in itself, all being mortal.

The practical S*irat-i-mustaqim*, concerning 'that which is due to one's fellow beings', consists in practicing genuine virtue, that is, doing that which is most beneficial and proper for them.

The theoretical *Sirat-al-mustaqîm*, in respect of 'that which is due to oneself', is that one should be aware of all the evils that spring from the ego, like self-estimation, ostentation, arrogance, spite, jealousy, vanity, greed, miserliness, negligence and injustice and should estimate them as degrading traits of character as they are in fact.

The practical *Sirat-al-mustaqîm*, concerning 'that which is due to oneself', is to purge one's self of all low inclinations, to be emptied of all dross and to be equipped with all excellent traits. This indeed is the straight course (*Sirat-al-mustaqîm*) in practice.

The practical aspect of *Sirat-al-mustaqîm* concerning one's fellow beings, is fulfilled only through service and the practical aspect of that which is due to oneself is realized through self-purification and does not necessarily call for any service. This self-purification can be achieved even in the solitude of wilderness. But that which is due to other human beings cannot be rendered except in the midst of one's fellow beings.

That is why it has been said that there is no monasticism in Islam. *(see Ch.57:Verse 27).*

It must, therefore, be understood that the meaning of *Sirat-al-mustaqîm*, both theoretical and practical is theoretical knowledge of *Tauhîd* and a life lived in terms of *Tauhîd,* that is, *Tauhîd* through knowledge and *Tauhîd* through practice. The Holy Qur'ân sets forth only one true objective, true Unity, all the rest being means towards achieving it.

**Sirat-al-mustaqîm is a great blessing and is the source of all gifts and the door to every bounty:** This verse indicates that *Sirat-al-mustaqîm* is a great blessing and is the source of all gifts and the door to every bounty. When a person is honored with this great kingdom and dominion that never decays, he becomes the recipient of favors upon favors. Whoso prepares himself for receiving this felicity and perseveres in the effort, is called to every type of guidance and enjoys a pleasant life and experiences an illuminating light, after nights of darkness. Allâh saves him from every slip, admits him into the company of the righteous, after he had been involved with the rebellious, and shows him the ways of those He favors, those who have not incurred His displeasure and have not gone astray.

**Sirat-al-mustaqîm objective of worshipper:** The reality of *Sirat-al-mustaqîm*, as designed in the firm Faith, is the worshiper's love for His gracious Lord, and his complete acceptance of the will of Allâh and committing his soul and his heart to Him. Dedicating his whole attention to Him Who created him, and praying to none but Him. Loving Allah with all his heart and supplicating Him alone and seeking His mercy and compassion, and emerging out of his stupor, and walking straight and fearing the Gracious Lord, His love permeating his whole being with Allâh helping him, strengthening his belief and faith.

The *Sirat-al-mustaqîm* is the end of the journey of the spiritual wayfarers, which is the final objective of the seekers and the worshippers. No mercy is bestowed until after this light descend, nor is any true success achieved except after it has been possessed.

This is the key by means of which the spiritual wayfarer expresses his innermost thoughts in his supplications to His Lord and whereby the gates of discernment are opened to him and He is made a *muhaddis* by the Most Forgiving Allâh. Whoso makes this supplication secretly in the morning with sincerity and pure intent, observing all the conditions of righteousness and loyalty, undoubtedly arrives at the station of the chosen and the elect and the elite.

**Worshipper should stand before Allâh with yearning and total humility:** One who heaves sighs, while supplicating the Bountiful Lord, like one who has lost his child, entreating acceptance of his prayer by Allâh, the Gracious, with humility and lowliness, while his eyes overflow with tears, his prayer is verily heard.

He is granted a position of honor and is vouchsafed appropriate guidance. His faith is strengthened with arguments resplendent like rubies and his heart, hitherto weaker than a spider's web, is fortified.

He is granted excellence of character and is enabled to observe minute details of piety. He is invited to the table of the spiritually exalted and to the pure provisions meant for the saintly. He overcomes at all times every desire, utilizing it under the superintendence of the law (*shari'ah*) as a vehicle to carry it wherever he wishes to go, like an expert rider bestriding a docile mount.

He desires not the world nor puts himself in hardship on account of it; nor does he grovel before its golden calf. Allâh is his Guardian and He indeed is the Guardian of the righteous. His mind is at rest, and has no tendency left to misguide him to his ruin. It no longer stares at the world like a hawk glaring at his prey from above.

He sees the goals of his journey clearly like the munificent; his generosity is not niggardly; he is a source of freshness for others, like clear running water. Allâh has urged His servants to seek of Him perseverance in striving for this position and steadfastness and ability to reach this eminence, for it is indeed a high position and an inaccessible objective, attainable by none except through the grace of their Lord and not at all through the exertions of their minds.

It is, therefore, necessary that the worshipper should proceed to the Presence of the Lord of Honor, yearning for this prize and beg of Him success in this endeavor, standing and bowing down and in prostration, groveling in the dust of humility as the mendicants and the hard-pressed keep supplicating with outstretched arms.

The prayer: 'Lead us on the exact right path till we reach the goal'; implies that when human effort reaches its limit, one has to turn to Allâh, the Exalted. A prayer is perfect when it comprises every good and safeguards against every evil. The prayer: 'Lead us on the exact right path till we reach the goal'; comprises every form of good; and: not of those who incurred Thy wrath nor of those who went astray; is a supplication to be safeguarded against every evil, including the wickedness of the Dissembler *(Dajjâl).*

**Sources of guidance for Muslims:** The Muslims have available to them the following sources of guidance towards the *Sirat-al-mustaqîm*;

(l) The Holy Qur'ân, the Book of Allâh. We have nothing more conclusive and certain than this, the Word of God, free from all doubt and vagueness;

(2) The *Sunnah*, that is, the practical example of the Holy Prophet, regarding the application of the teachings and principals of the Holy Qur'an. In other words, the Holy Qur'ân is the Word of God, the Exalted, and *Sunnah* is the practice of the Holy Prophet صلى الله عليه وسلم illustrating the teachings, commands and values propounded in the Holy Qur'ân. It is contemporaneous with the Holy Qur'ân and shall so remain.

It has ever been the way of Allâh that when the Messengers and Prophets (peace be on them all) communicate the revealed word of God for the guidance of people, they illustrate it in practice through personal example, so that its import may be clearly grasped, and make others practice it likewise.

**The ultimate object of human's creation is the worship and service of God:** This verse of the *Surah Al-Fâtihah* teaches the prayer: 'Lead us on the exact right path till we reach the goal'; that is, make us steadfast in the path of righteousness, the path of those who became the recipients of Thy bounties and for whom the gates of heaven were opened.

It must be remembered that steadfastness of attitude is determined with reference to the ultimate object of the creation of each species. The ultimate object of human's creation is the worship and service of God. The steadfastness of human, therefore, is that having been created for perpetual obedience to God.

When a person becomes wholly devoted to Him with all his powers and capacities, he is rewarded with what may be described as the pure and enlightened life.

Observe that when a window facing the sun is opened, its rays enter through the window. Similarly when a person faces up to God, the Supreme, and there is no intervening screen between him and God, the Sublime then at once a luminous light descends on him and illumines him and dispels all his inner uncleanliness. Then he becomes a new person and experiences a great change. It is then said that he has been given a pure and enlightened life. This change takes place in this very life.

It is to this that Allâh, the Lord of glory and honor, draws attention in the verse:[93]

وَمَنْ كَانَ فِي هَٰذِهِ أَعْمَىٰ فَهُوَ فِي الْآخِرَةِ أَعْمَىٰ وَأَضَلُّ سَبِيلًا (٧٢)

*But whoever remained (spiritually) blind in this world shall also be blind in the Hereafter. Rather he will be even farther removed from the right path. (17.72)*

**Worship should win Divine pleasure:** This prayer is taught so that we may not rest content with merely believing and should exert ourselves in pursuit of Divine favors with which the servants of God who approach close to Him are honored. There are many who fall into prostrations and offer prayers and observe other articles of faith but fail to win Divine help and support. There is no

[93] *The Holy Qur'ân: explained by 'Allamah Nooruddîn, rendered into English by Mrs. A. R. 'Omar; 'Abdul Mannân 'Omar*

noticeable change in their ways and habits, which shows that their acts of worship are mere form and lack its true essence and reality – we should do our best to be not of them.

Observance of Divine ordinances is like the sowing of a seed the sprouting of which affects both the soul and the body. If a person irrigates a field and works hard at sowing the seed but finds after a couple of months that it has not germinated at all, he concludes that the seed was defective. The same may be said of worship. If a person believes in the Unity of God, offers prayers, observes fasts and apparently carries out Divine ordinances to the best of his ability, yet no Divine support is extended to him, the conclusion is inevitable that the seed he is sowing is defective. In other words, all his acts of worship are mere form and lack true and healthy essence and reality.

Prayer should be such as to melt down the evil-prompting ego (*nafs e-amârah*) to a state of tranquility (*nafs e-mutma'inna*h). If one keeps up the supplication: 'Lead us along the exact right path path till we reach the goal'; (in the sense already explained) one's other needs for which one may wish to pray, will be fulfilled by God, InshAllâh.

**Salvation cannot be achieved through prayers and fasting alone:** The concept of salvation deducible from the Holy Qur'ân is that salvation is achieved neither through fasting and Prayer services nor through *Zakat* or almsgiving but only through Supplication and Grace of God.

That is why God, the Sublime, has taught the prayer: 'Guide us along the straight path'. When it is heard, it absorbs the grace of God. Good deeds are its accompaniment but not its essentials. When a prayer is accepted all necessary adjuncts fall into line.

Were salvation contingent on deeds, it would be a subtle form of confusion regarding the concept of God. It would mean that a person can work out his salvation by himself, for, deeds are voluntary and people perform them on their own. When prayer is offered with all its adjuncts, it absorbs Divine Grace and thereafter all conditions automatically start falling into line. This is the concept of salvation in Islam.

Prayer should be directed towards the seeking of the pleasure of God and freedom from sin. Everything else is included in it. 'Guide us along the straight path till we reach the goal', is a great prayer indeed. The straight path means, in other words, knowledge and worship of God; by safeguarding against sin and joining the company of the righteous.

The most cherished wish of a person in respect of this life is to enjoy ease and comfort. Allâh has appointed a way for it; it is called the way of righteousness. In other words, it is the way of the Holy Qur'ân, or the *Sirat-al-mustaqîm*, the straight and right path which lead us to the ultimate goal of success.

The essence and soul of communion is the prayer. When we supplicate: Lead us along the straight path till we reach the goal; we seek to draw by means of this prayer, the light that comes down from God, the Supreme, illuminating hearts with certainty and love.

Lead us; implies seeking knowledge; and perfection in practical implementation is indicated here: meaning thereby that the best and most perfect results may be attained.

A plant cannot bear flowers and fruits until it receives proper nourishment and growth. The same is true of guidance. If it does not produce perfect and excellent results, it is a dead direction, lacking in qualities and properties of growth.

In other words, this is not a barren, disconcerting and distracting path. On the contrary, one who treads along it attains to success and achieves his goal. The real goal that Allâh, the Supreme, has appointed for humanity is the path of the righteous and of the Divinely-favored.

**True prayer should aim at pleasing Allâh:** Miscellaneous prayers are secondary. True prayer should aim at pleasing Allâh, the Exalted; other prayers will be heard in consequence. Blessings come after sins disappear.

The prayer that is directed solely at some worldly objective is not proper. Therefore, we need to pray primarily to please Allâh and the best prayer for the purpose is: Lead us along the straight path till we reach the goal. Persistence in this prayer admits to the company of the favored ones immersed in the stream of Divine Love. Joining this party of dedicated ones the supplicant will receive Divine bounties as is the way of Allâh with such people.

Allâh, the Sublime, never condemns a faithful believer to destitution. In fact, Allâh is compassionate unto his seventh generation. The Holy Qur'ân relates the story of *Khidzar and Moses*. They unearthed a treasure in respect of which it was said that it had been saved for two orphans since their father was a righteous person. [94]

---

[94] *The Holy Qur'ân: explained by 'Allamah Nooruddîn, rendered into English by Mrs. A. R. 'Omar; 'Abdul Mannân 'Omar*

وَأَمَّا الْجِدَارُ فَكَانَ لِغُلَامَيْنِ يَتِيمَيْنِ فِي الْمَدِينَةِ وَكَانَ تَحْتَهُ كَنْزٌ لَهُمَا وَكَانَ أَبُوهُمَا صَالِحًا فَأَرَادَ رَبُّكَ أَنْ يَبْلُغَا أَشُدَّهُمَا وَيَسْتَخْرِجَا كَنْزَهُمَا رَحْمَةً مِنْ رَبِّكَ ۚ وَمَا فَعَلْتُهُ عَنْ أَمْرِي ۚ ذَٰلِكَ تَأْوِيلُ مَا لَمْ تَسْطِعْ عَلَيْهِ صَبْرًا (٨٢)

*`As for the wall it belonged to two orphan boys of the town and under this (wall there) was a treasure belonging to them and their father had been a righteous man. So your Lord desired that they should attain their (age of) full strength and then take out their treasure; a mercy from your Lord, and I did not do it of my own accord, (whatever I did was the will of the Lord). This is the significance of that which you were not able to bear with patience.' (18:82)*

This verse refers to the parents but does not say what sort of people the children were. The treasure was kept safe on account of the father and it was because of him that they were treated mercifully. Nothing is said in respect of the boys. God overlooked their faults.

The Torah and all the other sacred Books affirm that God does not let down the righteous. Therefore, one should first strive through prayer to convert the evil-prompting spirit into the tranquil spirit so that Allâh, the Glorious, is pleased. Therefore, take to the prayer: Guide us along the straight path till we reach the goal. For, once this has been heard, God grants of Himself whatever the worshipper needs.

**Hardships and trials must be encountered for winning the pleasure of Allâh:** When a service is appreciated by God a bounty is bestowed. The extraordinary signs and miracles which others are not able to duplicate are the bounties of God, the Supreme, which are bestowed on His servants.

Since, supplication is made for guidance along the way of the Prophets, henceforth be prepared for trials and tests and keep imploring Him for steadfastness.

One who wants to continue in good health and security, and desires increase of wealth and of all the means of pleasure and enjoyment and every type of comfort and luxury, unmarred by any trial and at the same time hopes to win the pleasure of God, is bereft of good sense. He can never succeed. Those who have succeeded in winning the pleasure of God had to go through trials of different kinds and encountered various types of hardship.

In brief' Allâh, the Exalted, has given us to understand that He is ready to give if we are ready to receive. This supplication is an indication of readiness to receive the guidance.

# Verse 7

صِرَاطَ الَّذِينَ أَنْعَمْتَ عَلَيْهِمْ غَيْرِ الْمَغْضُوبِ عَلَيْهِمْ وَلَا
الضَّالِّينَ (٧)

*The path of those on whom You have bestowed (Your) blessings, those who have not incurred (Your) displeasure, and those who have not gone astray.*

## Important Arabic Words Used In This Verse

***Sirât*** صراط; An'amta انعمتَ;
Maghdzûb مغضوب; Dzâlîn ضَّالِّينَ

***Sirât*** صراط: (Root Word ***Sirât*** صراط)

**Meanings:** A path which is even, wide enough and can be trodden without difficulty; Way that is straight so that all part of it are in orderly array and are properly adjusted to one another.[95] [96]

[95] *Dictionary of the Holy Qur'ân by 'Abdul Mannân 'Omar (page 313)*
[96] *Mufradât fi Gharâib al-Qur'ân by Al-Raghib*

The Arab Lexicologists do not regard a **PATH** as *Sirât* until it comprises the following five prominent features:
*i. Being the shortest*
*ii. Being broad in width for travellers*
*iii. Leading surely to the objective*
*iv. Rectitude (leading to rightness of principle or conduct)*
*v. As the road to the goal in the eyes of the wayfarers*[97]

***An'amta* انعمت**: (Root Word: *Na'ma* نَعَم)

**Meanings:** Blessings; Bliss; Pleasant and Plentiful; Abundance; Enormous; Intense; comfort and delight; Beneficence; Favour; To become well off; To be Gifted (with speech, talent, reason etc..); Prosperity; Joy; 'Ease, and conveniences of life'. [98]

The word In'âm انعام is used with reference to rational beings only.

***Maghdzûb* مغضوب**: (Root Word: *Ghadziba* غضب)

**Meanings:** Displeasure; Anger; Indignation; Wrath; Passion; Hot temper; Irritation. [99]

***Dzâlîn* ضَّالِّينَ**: (Root word *Dzalla* ضل)

**Meanings:** Go astray; To lose one's way; To lose the right way; Fail; Leave in error; Deviate; Deviate from true guidance; Misled from the right path; Wander away; Lurch (a sudden tip or roll to one extreme side); Seducer; Deluder; ...[100]

---

[97] *Dictionary of the Holy Qur'ân by 'Abdul Mannân 'Omar (page 313)*
[98] *Dictionary of the Holy Qur'ân by 'Abdul Mannân 'Omar (page 569-570)*
[99] *Dictionary of the Holy Qur'ân by 'Abdul Mannân 'Omar (page 404)*
[100] *Dictionary of the Holy Qur'ân by 'Abdul Mannân 'Omar (page 333-334)*

# Pearls of Wisdom

Reference from the Holy Qur'ân regarding the three key words used in this verse, namely: *An'amta* انعمت; *Maghdzûb* مغضوب; *Dzâlîn* ضَّالِّينَ.[101]

وَمَنْ يُطِعِ اللَّـهَ وَالرَّسُولَ فَأُولَٰئِكَ مَعَ الَّذِينَ أَنْعَمَ اللَّـهُ عَلَيْهِمْ مِنَ النَّبِيِّينَ
وَالصِّدِّيقِينَ وَالشُّهَدَاءِ وَالصَّالِحِينَ ۚ وَحَسُنَ أُولَٰئِكَ رَفِيقًا (٦٩)

*And those who obey Allâh and this perfect Messenger, it is these who are with those upon whom Allâh has bestowed His blessings (in this life and the Hereafter) - the Prophets, the Truthful (in their belief, words and deeds), and the Bearers of Testimony (to the truth of the religion of Allâh by their words and deeds), as well as the Martyrs, and the Righteous (who stick to the right course under all circumstances), and how excellent companions they are! (4: 69)*

اهْبِطُوا مِصْرًا فَإِنَّ لَكُمْ مَا سَأَلْتُمْ ۗ وَضُرِبَتْ عَلَيْهِمُ الذِّلَّةُ وَالْمَسْكَنَةُ وَبَاءُوا
بِغَضَبٍ مِنَ اللَّـهِ ۗ ذَٰلِكَ بِأَنَّهُمْ كَانُوا يَكْفُرُونَ بِآيَاتِ اللَّـهِ وَيَقْتُلُونَ النَّبِيِّينَ بِغَيْرِ
الْحَقِّ ۗ ذَٰلِكَ بِمَا عَصَوْا وَكَانُوا يَعْتَدُونَ (٦١)

*And lo! it so happened, they were smitten with abasement and destitution and they incurred the displeasure of Allâh.*

---

[101] *The Holy Qur'ân: explained by 'Allamah Nooruddîn, rendered into English by Mrs. A. R. 'Omar; 'Abdul Mannân 'Omar*

*That was because they denied the Messages of Allâh and sought to kill His Prophets unjustly and that was because they disobeyed and had been transgressing. (2:61)*

Allâh does not visit anyone with displeasure; on the contrary a person draws His displeasure through his own evil conduct. It means that because of his sinfulness and transgression, a person is alienated from Allâh. [102]

قُلْ يَا أَهْلَ الْكِتَابِ لَا تَغْلُوا فِي دِينِكُمْ غَيْرَ الْحَقِّ وَلَا تَتَّبِعُوا أَهْوَاءَ قَوْمٍ قَدْ ضَلُّوا مِنْ قَبْلُ وَأَضَلُّوا كَثِيرًا وَضَلُّوا عَنْ سَوَاءِ السَّبِيلِ (٧٧)

*Say, `O People of the Scripture! do not exaggerate in (the matter of) your religion falsely and unjustly, nor follow the fancies of a people <u>who had gone astray before (you) and had led many astray, and (now again) who have strayed</u> (5:77)*

Allâh is commanding us, to seek through prayer every type of guidance granted to the Prophets, the righteous, the martyrs and the virtuous. So that all the guidance that was revealed to them may also be revealed to us, but through following them and as a reflection in a mirror of that which was granted to them, and according to the measure of our respective capacities and resolves.

Since search for guidance and purification of self are not enough for the attainment of nearness to God, without the practical assistance available from the Prophets, leading divines and those rightly guided, Allâh, the Holy, did not confine His direction to the instruction: Guide us along the right path; but urged His worshipers, by His words: 'the

[102] *The Holy Qur'ân: explained by 'Allamah Nooruddîn, rendered into English by Mrs. A. R. 'Omar; 'Abdul Mannân 'Omar*

path of those on whom You have bestowed (Your) blessings'; to look for these rightly-instructed guides and leaders from among the diligent and the pure-souled, that is to say, the Messengers, and Prophets. Indeed they are ways of Divine guidance.

One who disregards them, certainly deprives himself of a bounty he had been offered, and draws away from the fountain of blessings. This isolation is far more serious than the severance of ties of kinship and blood-relationship. These personalities are the heralds of paradise.

Woe to him who turns away from the Divine Messengers and Prophets, and confines himself to eating and drinking. Messengers are the light of Allâh and through them the hearts of people are granted illumination and antidote for the poison of sins, and tranquility in agony and in the throes of death, and fortitude at the hour of departure from this world.

Do you imagine that anyone else could be like this noble group? Indeed not, by the Lord who caused the date-palm to sprout forth from a stone-seed. That is why, out of abundant compassion Allâh taught this prayer. Commanding the Muslims to seek of Him the way of those He had favored and bestowed blessing. This verse conveys clearly to people of understanding that the Muslims have been established in the footsteps of the Prophets; and the righteous, noble and virtuous worshipers of All-Mighty God Allâh.

Had there been no possibility of such resemblance and likeness, it would have been vain to seek the excellences achieved by those who have passed away and this prayer would have been meaningless.

Allâh's command that we should supplicate Him in the Prayer services, morn and eve: Guide us along the straight path; and that we should keep seeking the way of His favored and blessed ones, the Prophets and the Apostles. Allah has ordained it from the beginning that He will continue to raise among the Muslims righteous people who will walk in the footsteps of the Prophets and that He will make them spiritual and rightly guided *Khalifas* as He made *Khalifas* before among the children of Abraham. [103]

وَعَدَ اللَّهُ الَّذِينَ آمَنُوا مِنْكُمْ وَعَمِلُوا الصَّالِحَاتِ لَيَسْتَخْلِفَنَّهُمْ فِي الْأَرْضِ كَمَا اسْتَخْلَفَ الَّذِينَ مِنْ قَبْلِهِمْ وَلَيُمَكِّنَنَّ لَهُمْ دِينَهُمُ الَّذِي ارْتَضَىٰ لَهُمْ وَلَيُبَدِّلَنَّهُمْ مِنْ بَعْدِ خَوْفِهِمْ أَمْنًا ۚ يَعْبُدُونَنِي لَا يُشْرِكُونَ بِي شَيْئًا ۚ وَمَنْ كَفَرَ بَعْدَ ذَٰلِكَ فَأُولَٰئِكَ هُمُ الْفَاسِقُونَ (٥٥)

*Allâh has promised those of you who believe and do deeds of righteousness that surely, He will make them successors (vouchsafed with both spiritual and temporal leadership) on the earth as He made successors (from among) their predecessors, and that He will surely establish for them their Faith which He has approved for them, and that He will surely replace their state of fear with a state of security and peace. They will worship Me (alone) and they will not associate anything with Me. And those who show ingratitude for all the favours done to them after that (His promise is fulfilled), it is they who will be reckoned as the worst disobedient. (24:55)*

This is indeed the truth. Allâh had designed to combine in the Muslims all the excellences and moral qualities of the virtuous predecessors. It was this that called for the teaching of this prayer.

[103] *The Holy Qur'ân: explained by 'Allamah Nooruddîn, rendered into English by Mrs. A. R. 'Omar; 'Abdul Mannân 'Omar*

The Muslims have been named the most excellent people in the Qur'ân: [104]

كُنْتُمْ خَيْرَ أُمَّةٍ أُخْرِجَتْ لِلنَّاسِ تَأْمُرُونَ بِالْمَعْرُوفِ وَتَنْهَوْنَ عَنِ الْمُنْكَرِ وَتُؤْمِنُونَ بِاللَّـهِ ۗ (١١٠)

*You are the noblest people raised up for the good of humankind. You enjoin equity and forbid evil, and you believe truly in Allâh...(3:110)*

Nevertheless, excellence is attained only if deeds, faith, knowledge and insight continue to be fostered, and the pleasure of Allâh is sought continuously.

**It is a characteristic of true revelation that it expounds the meaning of the abstract terms employed in it:** Most certainly it is a characteristic of true revelation that it expounds the meaning of the abstract terms employed in it. For instance, the verse of the *Al-Fâtihah*: 'Lead us along the right path till we reach the goal, the path of those on whom You have bestowed (Your) blessings'; employs the abstract term, 'bestowing of blessings', which calls for an explanation.

This is furnished in the Holy Qur'ân where Allah, the Exalted, says: [105]

وَمَنْ يُطِعِ اللَّـهَ وَالرَّسُولَ فَأُولَٰئِكَ مَعَ الَّذِينَ أَنْعَمَ اللَّـهُ عَلَيْهِمْ مِنَ النَّبِيِّينَ
وَالصِّدِّيقِينَ وَالشُّهَدَاءِ وَالصَّالِحِينَ ۚ وَحَسُنَ أُولَٰئِكَ رَفِيقًا (٦٩)

*And those who obey Allâh and this perfect Messenger, it is these who are with those upon whom Allâh has bestowed*

[104] *The Holy Qur'ân: explained by 'Allamah Nooruddîn, rendered into English by Mrs. A. R. 'Omar; 'Abdul Mannân 'Omar*
[105] *ibid*

*His blessings (in this life and the Hereafter) - the Prophets, the Truthful (in their belief, words and deeds), and the Bearers of Testimony (to the truth of the religion of Allâh by their words and deeds), as well as the Martyrs, and the Righteous (who stick to the right course under all circumstances), and how excellent companions they are! (4:69).*

**Purifying grace of the Holy Prophet صلى الله عليه وسلم continues:** The supplication: 'Lead us on the exact right path till we reach the goal, the path of those on whom You have bestowed Your blessings'; also refutes some of the contemporary orientalists who believe that all spiritual grace and blessings have come to an end, and that no effort or exertion can produce any spiritual result, nor can anyone today be granted access to the blessings and fruits with which the favored ones were previously honored.

These people thus consider that the beneficence of the Holy Qur'ân is no longer effective, and do not believe any longer in the purifying grace of the Holy Prophet Muhammad (peace and blessings of Allâh be on him).

For, if not a single person can now be invested with the qualities of the favored ones then what is the purpose of making this supplication? That, however, is not so. It is a great error on the part of those who hold such views.

The door of Divine grace and bounties is still open as wide as it was before, but these bounties and gifts are procurable only through obedience to Allâh and the Holy Prophet Muhammad صلى الله عليه وسلم. One who claims to partake of spiritual blessings and heavenly light independently of obedience to the Holy Prophet Muhammad صلى الله عليه وسلم is utterly false in his claim.

**Four grades of excellence:** There are four examples of excellence mentioned in the Holy Qur'ân. It is the duty of every believer to aspire after. One who has no part in them at all, is devoid of faith. That is why Allâh, the Lord of glory, has appointed for Muslims the prayer: 'Lead us on the exact right path till we reach the goal, the path of those on whom You have bestowed Your blessings', so that they should keep supplicating for these favors and blessings. The Holy Qur'ân explains that the favored and the blessed ones are the Prophets, the righteous, the martyrs and the virtuous.

The Holy Qur'ân says:[106]

وَمَنْ يُطِعِ اللَّهَ وَالرَّسُولَ فَأُولَٰئِكَ مَعَ الَّذِينَ أَنْعَمَ اللَّهُ عَلَيْهِمْ مِنَ النَّبِيِّينَ
وَالصِّدِّيقِينَ وَالشُّهَدَاءِ وَالصَّالِحِينَ ۚ وَحَسُنَ أُولَٰئِكَ رَفِيقًا (٦٩)

*And those who obey Allâh and this perfect Messenger, it is these who are with those upon whom Allâh has bestowed His blessings (in this life and the Hereafter) - the Prophets, the Truthful (in their belief, words and deeds), and the Bearers of Testimony (to the truth of the religion of Allâh by their words and deeds), as well as the Martyrs, and the Righteous (who stick to the right course under all circumstances), and how excellent companions they are! (4:69).*

This prayer is offered in each *raka'a* of each formal Prayer service. Its very repetition emphasizes its significance. We should bear in mind that this is not a matter of small import and that it is not enough merely to repeat these words by

---

[106] *The Holy Qur'ân: explained by 'Allamah Nooruddîn, rendered into English by Mrs. A. R. 'Omar; 'Abdul Mannân 'Omar*

rote. In fact, it is an efficacious and unfailing instrument for converting a person into an ideal human being.

Once again, it should never be forgotten that some parts of the Holy Qur'ân explain its other parts. A subject finds a summary mention in one place and is explained at length in another. Thus: Guide us along the straight path, the path of those on whom Thou hast bestowed favors; is a supplication in the abstract. As mentioned above in (4: 69), the favored and blessed ones have been described as the Prophets, the righteous, the martyrs and the virtuous. The Prophets comprise the excellences of all four categories. For this is the apex of perfection.

It is the duty of every one to cultivate these excellences through appropriate exertions, in the way the Holy Prophet ﷺ and his righteous Companions(RZ) demonstrated through their example. [107]

وَالسَّابِقُونَ الْأَوَّلُونَ مِنَ الْمُهَاجِرِينَ وَالْأَنصَارِ وَالَّذِينَ اتَّبَعُوهُم بِإِحْسَانٍ رَّضِيَ اللَّهُ عَنْهُمْ وَرَضُوا عَنْهُ وَأَعَدَّ لَهُمْ جَنَّاتٍ تَجْرِي تَحْتَهَا الْأَنْهَارُ خَالِدِينَ فِيهَا أَبَدًا ۚ ذَٰلِكَ الْفَوْزُ الْعَظِيمُ (١٠٠)

*And (as for) the foremost (in spiritual rank, outstripping others in faith and righteous actions) and the first (to embrace Islam) from among the Emigrants and the Helpers and those who followed their example in the best possible manner, Allâh is well-pleased with them and they are well-pleased with Him, He has provided for them Gardens served with running streams (to keep them green and flourishing). They will abide therein forever. That indeed is the most sublime achievement.. (9:100)*

[107] *The Holy Qur'ân: explained by 'Allamah Nooruddîn, rendered into English by Mrs. A. R. 'Omar; 'Abdul Mannân 'Omar*

**A comprehensive prayer should comprise of benefit and should safeguard against all evil and harm:** If you reflect, you will find that Allâh, the Sublime, has taught in these verses the prayer: 'Lead us on the exact right path till we reach the goal, the path of those on whom You have bestowed Your blessings' those who have not incurred (Your) displeasure, and those who have not gone astray'.

A comprehensive prayer should comprise every type of advantage and benefit and should safeguard against all evil and harm'. This prayer comprises every possible benefit and safeguards against every possible harm.

In truth Al-Islam is a faith, a follower of which rises high enough to shake hands with the angels. Were that not so, there would be no purpose in the supplication: 'Lead us on the exact right path till we reach the goal, the path of those on whom You have bestowed Your blessings'. This is not a supplication only for worldly benefits; spiritual bounties are thereby solicited as well.

**Allâh intends to prepare a community like the community prepared by the Holy Prophet صلى الله عليه وسلم :** It is the true purpose of every person to attain to the excellences of the favored and blessed ones to which Allâh, the Exalted, has called attention in: 'the path of those on whom You have bestowed Your blessings'. There should always be a community among Muslims, who should address itself particularly to this. For, by instituting this, Allâh, the Exalted, means to prepare a people like the people prepared by the Holy Prophet صلى الله عليه وسلم, so that the community in question may stand as a witness to the truth and magnificence of the Holy Qur'ân and the Holy Prophet صلى الله عليه وسلم.

Prophets are not sent to be worshipped. On the contrary, they are appointed by Allah so that people may pattern their lives according to their example and cultivate affinities with them and should identify themselves with them totally.

Allâh the Exalted says: [108]

قُلْ إِنْ كُنْتُمْ تُحِبُّونَ اللَّـهَ فَاتَّبِعُونِي يُحْبِبْكُمُ اللَّـهُ وَيَغْفِرْ لَكُمْ ذُنُوبَكُمْ ۗ وَاللَّـهُ غَفُورٌ رَحِيمٌ (٣١)

*Say, `Follow me if you love Allâh, (if you do so) Allâh will love you and grant you protection from your sins. Allâh is Great Protector, Ever Merciful.' (3:31)*

Allah will not withhold any blessing from one whom He loves. The true following of the Holy Prophet Muhammad صلى الله عليه وسلم, also means self-obliteration in obedience, which promotes one to the status of complete resemblance in faith and moral conduct.

The grace and beneficence is attainable only through Divine bounty. We believe that it is not possible even to stir a finger without the support and grace of God, the Exalted. It is, however, a person's duty to exert as far as he can and for this also to seek strength from Allah. Never losing hope in the process. A believer never despairs of God's mercy, as God, the Supreme, has said: Only the disbelievers' despair of the mercy of Allâh.

[108] *The Holy Qur'ân: explained by 'Allamah Nooruddîn, rendered into English by Mrs. A. R. 'Omar; 'Abdul Mannân 'Omar*

ا بَنِيَّ اذْهَبُوا فَتَحَسَّسُوا مِنْ يُوسُفَ وَأَخِيهِ وَلَا تَيْأَسُوا مِنْ رَوْحِ اللَّهِ ۖ إِنَّهُ لَا يَيْأَسُ مِنْ رَوْحِ اللَّهِ إِلَّا الْقَوْمُ الْكَافِرُونَ (٨٧)

*`Go, my sons, and make a thorough search for Joseph and his brother. Do not despair of Allâh's soothing mercy. Verily, none but the people who deny (the truth) can ever lose hope of Allâh's soothing mercy.' (12:87)*

Despair is a great evil. One who despairs in effect entertains an ill concept of God, the Exalted. Remember, most evils and vices spring from mistrust. Allâh, the Most High, has therefore, warned against it emphatically: Mistrust may cause great harm.

It is only the Qur'ân that has taught at the very outset the prayer to its readers and given them this hope, namely; Guide us along the way to those bounties, which Thou didst bestow on those who preceded us from among the Prophets, the righteous, the martyrs and the virtuous.

**Look up then and turn not down the invitation of the Qur'ân:** Look up then and turn not down the invitation of the Qur'ân, for, it means to grant us the gifts that were granted to those who have gone before. Let's go forward, therefore, in sincerity, truth, righteousness and love of Allâh, making this our sole purpose, as long as life lasts. Allâh will then honor whomsoever of us He wills.

By transfer of Prophethood from the house of Israel, Allâh, the Exalted, intended to demonstrate the honor and grace that He bestowed on the Holy Prophet Muhammad *(pbuh)*. This means: Allâh, favor us with the gifts and bounties that Thou didst confer on former Prophets and the righteous, the martyrs and the virtuous. It means: Lord, grant us the approach to Your nearness and love and knowledge that

You did granted to the Prophets and the holy ones and the pious.

It does not behoove a believer to lose heart. Progress towards higher grades in nearness to the Divine has no limit. It is a great mistake to limit something to a particular person, nationality or race.

One who comes to Allâh with a true heart does not go back empty-handed. What is needed is a pure mind. If those gifts and bounties are no longer to be bestowed on anyone then what is the purpose of making this supplication repeatedly in the five daily Prayer services?

If, as some people consider it a great virtue, the sole aim were to avoid the major sins, then the prayer to be included among the favored ones would not have been taught; the ultimate stage of which is dialogue between God and human. The excellence of the Prophets (peace upon all of them) was not confined merely to abstention from stealing and burglary. In fact, they had no peer in their love of God, and in sincerity and loyalty to Him.

God thus taught through this prayer that righteousness and Divine favor are the highest grade of virtue and until a person acquires these he is not considered virtuous or righteous and is not included among the favored and blessed ones.

The very beauty and charm of Islam lie in the fact that its blessings and its grace and the fruits of its pure teachings are ever available in abundance. This is the belief of all the Sufi Saints - great spiritual scholars of the faith. In fact they affirm that no one is a perfect follower of the Holy Prophet Muhammad صلى الله عليه وسلم unless he assimilates his moral and ethical excellences in his own personas as reflection. This is indeed true. For it is necessary for perfect obedience to the Holy Prophet صلى الله عليه وسلم that its fruits should be reaped.

When a person becomes fully obedient and completely effaces himself in submission to the Holy Prophet (blessings and peace of Allâh be on him) his state is comparable to that of a mirror placed right in front which receives and reproduces a complete reflection.

**It is in this sense that the divines have been called heirs of the Prophets:** By teaching this prayer: Guide us and lead us along the straight path, the path of those on whom Thou hast bestowed Thy favors and blessings; He gave to all true seekers the glad tidings that they could attain, through obedience to the chosen Prophet Muhammad صلى الله عليه وسلم, the formal, as well as the spiritual knowledge that was bestowed directly on other Prophets. It is in this sense that the divines have been called heirs of the Prophets. If they cannot inherit the spiritual insights then how can they be true heirs?

This verse is most marvelous; if it is mere empty words and God will not grant it, then why did He teach us such expressions? If we are not eligible for that station, why do we bother for nothing five times every day?

But Allâh is not niggardly; nor do Prophets appear so that they may be worshipped; they are sent to teach that those who would follow them would become their spiritual reflections.

That prayer is comprehensive which comprises all good and secures against all loss and injury. This prayer covers all possible benefits and safeguards against all harm that could undo a person.

**Three aspects of prayer – comprising mercy for all humanity:** In respect of prayer it should be remembered that in this *Al-Fâtihah,* Allâh, the Exalted, has taught the supplication: 'Guide **us** along the straight path, the path of those on whom You have bestowed Your blessings'. In respect of it three aspects should be kept in mind; namely, that one should include in it all people, all the Muslims and Non-Muslims. By such intent all humanity will be included in the prayer and that is what Allâh, the Supreme, desires.

For, in the preceding verses of this Surah He has named Himself ***RABB AL-'Âlamîn*** رَبِّ الْعَالَمِين Lord of Universal Providence, which urges towards universal compassion even including the beasts. Next He has named Himself *Al-Rahmân*, the Gracious One, which urges towards sympathy with all humanity, for *Rahmâniyyat* includes all humanity in its ambit. Then He has called Himself *Al-Rahîm* the Compassionate. This attribute promotes compassion for believers, for *Rahîmiyyat* is confined to the believers. Finally, He has named Himself Master of the Day of Requital, which urges towards compassion for the company present. For, the Day of Requital is the Day when companies will be present before God, the Supreme.

The supplication: Guide **us** along the straight path, thus takes into account all these categories. This arrangement shows that the prayer comprises mercy for all humanity; and this is the Islamic principle, that a Muslim should be the well-wisher of all.

**The favored ones and those smitten by God's displeasure will continue to exist:** The two other groups mentioned in contradistinction to the 'Favored and Blessed ones' are those 'Who incurred His displeasure and those who went astray'.

Many former peoples were lost because of their blindness towards knowledge of Allâh's attributes and His bounties and His pleasure. They passed their time in sinful pursuits and thus earned God's displeasure and they were smitten with humiliation and were counted among the lost. It is to them that Allâh pointed in His words: Those who incurred Thy displeasure and have gone astray.

In this very verse, the supplication is made to Allah, the Supreme, to seek protection against these misguided groups. When the whole of this prayer is offered together, that is, when the supplication is made: Lord, include us among the blessed ones and safeguard us against being included among those who were smitten by Thy displeasure, or those who have gone astray; it is understood that there is within God's knowledge a party of the favored ones who are contemporaries of those who incurred His displeasure and of those who went astray.

'Guide us along the straight path, the path of those on whom Thou hast bestowed Thy favors and blessings, not of those who have incurred Thy displeasure, nor of those who have gone astray'; clearly indicates that differences will continue till the end, there will always be the favored ones and also those under displeasure, but that false creeds will be vanquished through reasoning, argument of wisdom and the good example.

Since those who were smitten by His displeasure are undoubtedly the people who rejected Prophet Muhammad *(pbuh)* and called him an impostor and insulted him, equally without a doubt, there is in contrast with them a party of the favored ones who are faithful believers in the Holy Messenger Muhammad صلى الله عليه وسلم, honor him with dutiful hearts and are his helpers and witnesses before the world.

Until a person has laid up a treasure of righteous deeds he is not a believer. That is why God, the Supreme, has taught the prayer: 'Lead us along the straight path till we reach the goal', so that one may not confine virtuous activity merely to abandonment of major vices like theft, adultery, etc. By pointing to the ways of the favored ones, He has emphasized that righteousness and Divine favor are the highest grade of virtue and until a person attains to them, he cannot be considered virtuous.

God, the Sublime, did not teach the prayer: Do not include us among the law-breakers and the rebellious; and leave it there. He taught us to pray for being included among the favored ones and not among those who incurred Divine displeasure, nor among those who went astray.

**The Camphor Elixir and the Ginger Elixir:** We are instructed to pray not to be included among those who incurred Divine displeasure nor among those who went astray. This has been explained in another place in the Holy Qur'ân that the perfect development of a believer's soul takes place by means of two kinds of elixir, one is termed the 'camphor elixir' and the other is labeled the 'ginger elixir'.

When the 'camphor elixir' is taken, the ego cools down and loses all inclination towards evil, as camphor has the property of dissipating all toxic elements and so does this camphor elixir dissipate the poison of sin and mischief and neutralizes and suppresses the elements that being aroused work the ruin of the person. The other drink is the ginger elixir by means of which a person gains strength and vitality to perform acts of virtue and warmth is generated for that purpose.

Guide us and lead us along the right path till we reach the goal, the path of those on whom Thou hast bestowed Thy favors and blessings; is then the real objective and aim. This, in a manner of speaking, is the 'ginger elixir': and not of those who incurred Thy displeasure nor of those who went astray; is the 'camphor elixir'.

These verses indicate that the full development of a believer's soul is achieved when he takes two elixirs. First, he should take the camphor elixir. It cools down the evil inclinations of the ego. Camphor has the property of neutralizing poisonous matter. In the same way this camphor elixir dissipates the inner poison of sin and evil. And then he should drink the ginger elixir which gives one the strength to perform good and noble deeds.

That is why the supplication: The path of those on whom You have bestowed (Your) blessings, those who have not incurred (Your) displeasure, and those who have not gone astray. has been taught in this verse, whereby both the elixirs have been begged of Allâh, the Exalted.

This is the supplication that is made in every *raka'a* of every Prayer service. Its very repetition stresses its importance. All Muslims should remember that this is no ordinary matter; And that the mere parrot-like repetition of the words is not what is required. In fact this prayer is an unfailing and efficacious prescription for making a person perfect and it should be kept constantly in mind, as the noble objective and as a sure safeguard against sin.

**Allâh treats each person according to his attitude towards Him:** The explanation of these three verities is that people fall into three categories in respect of their professions, activities, conduct and motives. Some seek Allah with a true heart and turn to Him with humility and in sincerity. Then Allâh also seeks them and turns to them with mercy and grace. This is the state of Divine favor and blessing. This is conveyed in: 'The way of Thy favored and blessed ones'. These follow an even and straight path which qualifies them for the grace of Divine mercy, and since there remains no barrier between them and God and they are juxtaposed directly to Divine compassion, the light of Divine grace starts pouring in on them.

The second category is those who are deliberately hostile and turn their backs on Allâh like enemies. Then Allâh also turns His back on them and would not turn to them with compassion, the reason being that the hostility, disgust, anger, malevolence and dislike embedded in their hearts against Allâh become a barrier between Him and them. This state is 'the state of Divine displeasure'. It is to these that the Divine words: 'Not of those who incurred Your displeasure'; refer to.

The third category of people are those who are indifferent towards Allâh and do not seek Him with eagerness and effort. Allâh too disregards them and would not lead them to His way, for, they are slack in seeking it and do not care to qualify for the grace that has been appointed in the eternal law of Allâh for those who strive and work hard in seeking Him. This is designated as 'the state of Divine misguidance', meaning that Allâh adjudges them lost, as they did not seek the ways of guidance by effort and hard work and Allâh, in terms of His eternal law, did not grant them guidance and withheld from them His support. They are referred to in: 'Nor of those who have gone astray'.

The essence of these three verities is that Allâh treats each person according to his attitude towards Him. With those who are pleased with Him and seek Him with true love of heart and sincerity, He also is pleased and He sheds on them the light of His pleasure. But those who turn away from Him and deliberately choose to be hostile to Him, He too treats them accordingly. Towards those who are slack and neglectful in seeking Him, God also is indifferent and He leaves them in their misguidance.

In brief, as human being observes his face in a mirror and beholds it as it really is. Similarly the One God loves those who love Him, is displeased and angry with those who are displeased and angry with Him, disregards those who disregard Him, withholds Himself from those who keep away from Him, inclines towards those who incline towards Him and dislikes those who dislike Him. As you behold in a mirror the attitude you adopt in front of it, likewise shall one find reflected from Allah the attitude one adopts towards Him. The garments a person put on are reflected back. He reaps what he sows.

When a person disencumbers his heart of all barriers and dirt and defilement and the expanse of his heart is cleansed of all base matters that divide him from the Divine, he is like the person who opens his door which faces the sun and its rays pour in through it.

But when a person takes to untruth, falsehood and different kinds of filth, and discards God as a thing scorned, he is like one who dislikes light and has such aversion towards it that he shuts all the doors of his house lest the rays of the sun should find their way into it from some direction.

When because of passion or considerations of honor and prestige or for the sake of alignment with his people a person becomes involved in different kinds of errors and filth and makes no effort and takes no pains to cleanse himself of these corruptions, on account of indolence, negligence and indifference, his case is like that of one who finds all the doors of his house closed and the entire house plunged in utter darkness but would not make a move to open the doors and sits inert, disinclined to stir.

**Divine displeasure means loss of Divine mercy:** These three descriptions illustrate the three conditions of a person that are the products of his own activity or inactivity. Of these, as explained before, the first is called the state of Divine favor and blessing, the second the state of Divine displeasure and the third the state of Divine misguidance.

Some people have no inkling of these three verities. For instance, some have no idea at all of the verity that makes Allâh, the Sublime, to treat with displeasure the rebellious and the malignant.

One such person has published a pamphlet on this subject. The writer in the course of it criticizes the Books of Allâh for ascribing the attribute of anger to the Divine-Being. Is God chagrined at our short-comings, he asks?

It is obvious that if the writer knew aught of this verity he would not have wasted his time in composing such a pamphlet as discloses his lack of insight. With all his pretensions to knowledge he has failed to realize that Allâh's displeasure is but a reflection of a person's own attitude.

When a person is enveloped in wicked hostility and turns his back on Allâh, does he still remain worthy of the grace of mercy that the true adorers and sincere devotees receive? Indeed not. On the contrary, the eternal law of God which the righteous have throughout experienced and still continue to experience ordains that one who, emerging from behind dark barriers, runs straight to God, with his soul wholly turned to Him, in prostration at His porch, becomes the recipient of the special grace of Divine compassion. One who turns in a different direction, experiences inevitably Divine displeasure which is the negation of Divine Mercy.

The true nature of Divine displeasure is the state of loss of Divine mercy, otherwise termed the state of Divine displeasure. When a person abandons the right path which is the means of receiving Divine mercy, under Divine law, he, as a consequence, forfeits Divine grace.
Since life and comfort and tranquility are due to the grace of God, those who discard the way to the grace of mercy, are afflicted with sufferings of different kinds in this life or in the hereafter, for the simple reason that one who does not enjoy Divine compassion, inevitably draws upon himself different types of spiritual and physical afflictions.

"As regards the two categories of people following a wrong course, some of the greatest Islamic thinkers (e.g., Al-Ghazali or, in recent times, Muhammad 'Abduh) held the view that the people described as having incurred "God's condemnation" - that is, having deprived themselves of His grace - are those who have become fully cognizant of God's message and, having understood it, have rejected it; while by "those who go astray" are meant people whom the truth has either not reached at all, or to whom it has come in so garbled and corrupted a form as to make it difficult for them to recognize it as the truth (see 'Abduh in Manâr I, 68 ff.)" [109]

"Note that the words relating to Grace are connected actively with Allah; those relating to Wrath are impersonal. In the one case Allah's Mercy encompasses us beyond our

[109] *The Message of the Qur'ân: Translated and Explained by Muhammad Asad, ed.1984 (page2)*

deserts. In the other case our own actions are responsible for the Wrath-the negative of Grace, Peace, or Harmony.

Are there two categories? those who are in the darkness of Wrath and those who stray? The first are those who deliberately break Allah's law; the second those who stray out of carelessness or negligence. Both are responsible for their own acts or omissions.

In opposition to both are the people who are in the light of Allah's Grace: for His Grace not only protects them from active wrong (if they will only submit their will to Him) but also from straying into paths of temptation or carelessness..."[110]

It is part of Divine law that special grace is bestowed on those who take to the path of mercy, namely that of prayer and Unity. Consequently those who disregard that path are afflicted with various kinds of calamities.

This is indicated in the Holy Qura'an: [111]

قُلْ مَا يَعْبَأُ بِكُمْ رَبِّي لَوْلَا دُعَاؤُكُمْ ۖ فَقَدْ كَذَّبْتُمْ فَسَوْفَ يَكُونُ لِزَامًا (٧٧)

*Say (to the disbelievers), `My Lord will not hold you to be of any worth if you do not call on Him (in your prayers seeking His protection). Since you cried lies (to the word of God), so you must now encounter a lasting punishment.' (25:77)*

Yes, Allâh is Independent and depends not on anything what so ever. [112]

---

[110] *The Meaning of the Holy Qur'ân by 'Abdullah Yûsuf 'Alî, Tenth Edition (page 15).*

[111] *The Holy Qur'ân: explained by 'Allamah Nooruddîn, rendered into English by Mrs. A. R. 'Omar; 'Abdul Mannân 'Omar*

[112] *ibid*

... وَمَنْ كَفَرَ فَإِنَّ اللَّـهَ غَنِيٌّ عَنِ الْعَالَمِينَ (٩٧)

*... And whosoever disobeys (let him remember that) Allâh is Independent of the worlds. (3:97).*

**In accord with His eternal law, Allâh treats everyone according to his deserts:** Some people ask why Allâh would not guide everyone and some object why Allâh should have the attribute of misguidance.

Those who ask about Divine guidance do not realize that Divine guidance is accorded only to those who strive for it and walk the way that one must walk to have Divine grace. Those who object to Divine misguidance do not reflect that, in accord with His eternal law, Allâh treats everyone according to his deserts. Those who would not strive after Him because of indolence and negligence He deprives of His support. This is His eternal way. He guides along His ways only those who seek them sincerely and earnestly.

How can it be possible that one who is negligent and full of utter disregard should be blessed with Divine grace in the same way as one who seeks Him with all his wisdom and strength and sincerity! This is indicated in: [113]

وَالَّذِينَ جَاهَدُوا فِينَا لَنَهْدِيَنَّهُمْ سُبُلَنَا ۚ وَإِنَّ اللَّـهَ لَمَعَ الْمُحْسِنِينَ (٦٩)

*We surely guide along Our ways those who strive after Us (29:69).*

**Every human action is followed by Divine reaction:** It is not by way of a story or a fable that Allâh imparted this teaching. On the contrary, He knew that as former peoples practiced vice and rejected the Prophets and exceeded all

[113] ibid

limits in delinquency, so shall the Muslims pass through a period when they will indulge in vice and transgression, violating all boundaries and will take to practices which inflamed the displeasure of God against former peoples and shall likewise incur His displeasure.

Few commentators have designated some particular Jews of the past, as the people who had incurred Divine displeasure. For some of the Jews had subjected the Prophets of Allâh to much ridicule. Some of them had been particularly harsh towards Jesus (peace be on him) indulging in great impertinence and insolence. The consequence of which was that they were afflicted with Divine displeasure in this very world.

The expression Divine displeasure should not be construed to mean that God is chagrined against people. It means that because of his sinfulness a person is alienated from God, irrespective of creed, ethnicity, religion or gender.

For example, take the case of a person who occupies a chamber that has four doors. If he keeps them open, sunlight would pour in. But should he shut all the doors then light would not find its way into the chamber.

The truth of the matter is that it is the way of Allâh that every human action is followed by a Divine reaction. When this person unfortunately for himself shut all the four doors of his chamber, the Divine reaction is that the chamber is plunged into darkness. This plunging into darkness is termed 'Divine displeasure'.

# Synopsis

## ESSENCE & BEAUTY OF SURAH AL-FÂTIHAH

This is the purport of *Al-Fâtihah* which Muslims recite in their five daily Prayer services. In fact, this very supplication is the essence of Prayer and until one recites it with an aching heart in the Presence of All Mighty God - Allâh, and seeks the unraveling of the knot for which this supplication has been taught, one has, in fact, not performed the Prayer.

"By universal consent it is rightly placed at the beginning of the Quran, as summing up, in marvelously terse and comprehensive words, man's relation to Allah in contemplation and prayer. In our spiritual contemplation the first words should be those of praise. If the praise is from our inmost being, it brings us into union with Allah's Will. Then our eyes see all good, peace, and harmony. Evil, rebellion, and conflict are purged out. They do not exist for us, for our eyes are lifted up above them in praise. Then we see Allah's attributes better (verses 2-4). This leads us to the attitude of worship and acknowledgment (verse 5). And finally comes prayer for guidance, and a contemplation of what guidance means (verses 6-7).

Allah needs no praise, for He is above all praise; He needs no petition, for He knows our needs better than we do ourselves; and His bounties are open without asking, to the righteous and the sinner alike. The prayer is for our own spiritual education, consolation, and confirmation.

That is why the words in this Surah are given to us in the form in which we should utter them. When we reach enlightenment, they flow spontaneously from us."[114]

## Three lessons have been taught in this Prayer:

**First**, the Unity of the All Mighty God - Allâh and His attributes, so that His worshipper may turn wholly away from the sun, the moon, and all other false deities, to the worship of the One true God and that his soul may cry out: 'You alone do we worship and You alone do we implore for help'.

**Secondly**, he has been taught to include his fellow human beings in his prayers and thus to discharge his debt to humanity. The supplication is in the plural: Lead **us** along the straight path; and not merely: Lead **me** along the straight path.

**Thirdly**, the object of the supplication is to implore that He may not leave our faith at the theoretical level of mere verbal affirmation but may be pleased to bestow upon us spiritual bounties that He conferred upon the righteous in the past. We are also directed to pray, at the same time, that He may safeguard us against the way of those who were not granted spiritual sight and who indulged in practices that brought down displeasure upon them in this world or who were saved from displeasure in this world but died in misguidance and were involved in punishment in the hereafter.

The purport of this prayer is that if Allâh would not grant a person spiritual favors and seeing eyes and would not fill his heart with certainty and insight he is doomed in the end;

---

[114] *The Meaning of the Holy Qur'ân by 'Abdullah Yûsuf 'Alî, Tenth Edition (page 14).*

and because of his insolence and wickedness he is punished in this very world, for he takes to slandering the righteous, and act in other wicked ways and is, therefore, annihilated as were the some nations in the past, because of their wickedness and impertinence, and were afflicted time and again with the scourge of plague and other warnings and punishments which utterly ruined them.

If a person does not **act** wickedly and insolently in this world and does not lend himself to campaigns of slander and mischief, but he does not believe in the true faith, his chastisement is merely postponed to the next world after he has passed away from this world. In short, Allâh does not punish a person in this world only because of his belief system. The judgment of the wrong belief system is solely reserved for the next world.

All praise and all true and perfect praise and glorification belong admittedly and exclusively to the Almighty God - Allâh, the Creator, Sustainer and Guardian-Evolver of everything. There is not a thing that is not created by Him and that He does not sustain and evolve.

He is the most Gracious *(Al-Rahmân)*, that is, He bestows bounties upon His servants, believers and non-believers alike, without reference to their deeds and has already granted them innumerable gifts for their well-being and comfort. He is the Compassionate and Merciful, that is, first through His *Rahmâniyyat*, which is not actuated by any effort on the part of man, He grants people such powers and faculties as enable them to do good deeds and provides all kinds of means for the perfection of deeds, and when through the grace of His being *Al-Rahim (Ever Merciful)* a person is enabled to perform good deeds, then for enabling him to merit reward for his deeds. As the other name of Allâh is *Al-Rahîm.*

When through the grace of His *Rahîmiyyat* a person is qualified to receive lasting gifts and honors, then for the award of this everlasting reward and honor the name of God, the Sublime, is Supreme Master of the Day of Requital *(Mâlik-e-Youmiddîn).* As He is the Supreme Master, he can forgive us our sins and can multiply the rewards many times over.

After this, He directs us to supplicate: O Allâh Who art the aggregate of these attributes, we worship Thee alone and for this worship and for doing other good works we seek only Thy help. Guide us and lead us along the right path till we reach our goal, the path of those on whom Thou hast bestowed favors and blessings. And safeguard us against following the way of those who are under Thy displeasure, who behave with such arrogance and wickedness that they are afflicted with chastisement in this very life. And safeguard us against following the path of those who lost Thy way and have taken to paths that are not approved by Thee.

Observe then how this *Surah* (Chapter) of the Holy Qur'ân, called *Surah Al-Fâtihah*, brims over with teachings on the Unity of the Divine Being. There is nowhere in it any claim on the part of a human that he is self-existent, nor that his deeds derive from his own power and potential. The supplication is: Guide us and lead us along the path by following which a person finds Thee and earns Thy spiritual and worldly rewards and honors and is safeguarded against Thy displeasure and against going astray.

This *Surah* indicates the blessings of prayer and emphasizes that all good things descend from heaven and that one who recognizes the truth and is firmly established in guidance and is disciplined and becomes righteous will never be let down by Allâh and will be admitted by Him among His favored and blessed servants, and whoso disobeys Him will be lost and ruined.

**Divine attributes operate in proportion to supplicant's faith:** This *Surah* points out that the fortunate one is he who is eager for prayer and is never tired of praying nor frowns on it nor despairs and relies firmly on the grace of his Lord until His benevolence favors him and he is numbered among the successful.

This *Surah* also indicates that the attributes of Allâh the Most High, are operative in proportion to the degree of a servant's faith in them. When a discerning one contemplates an attribute of Allâh, the Exalted, and perceives Him with the eye of his soul and believes and continues to advance in faith until he is totally immersed in his faith, the spiritual essence of the attribute pervades his heart and takes possession of it. The seeker then finds emptied of all except the Gracious Lord, his heart is at rest with faith; his life is sweetened by the remembrance of the Beneficent and he becomes one of the happy and blessed ones.

Then he experiences further manifestations of that attribute until his heart becomes the throne of the attribute and he is dyed in its hues and color after the removal of all trace of his ego and his total devotion to Him.

*Surah Al-Fâtihah* furnishes this indication in its very opening phrase: All true and perfect praise belongs to Allâh alone.

Allâh, the Supreme, does not command us here: Proclaim: All praise belongs to Allâh; but simply affirms: All true praise and glory belongs to Allâh alone. In other words

Allâh makes human nature affirm this truth and thus discloses to us what is inherent in our nature.

This shows that the human nature is in accord with *Al-Islam* and that it is in his nature to render praise to Allâh, the Sublime, and to believe Him to be the Lord of universal providence, the Gracious, the Compassionate the Merciful and Master of the Day of Requital; and that He helps those who seek His help and guides those who supplicate Him.

It is thus established that insight into the Divine and His worship have been embedded in human nature and that His love has been infused in the human heart. But this state is revealed after the intervening veils have been lifted and then the remembrance of Allâh, the Most High, becomes the spontaneous occupation of the tongue, the tree of divine knowledge is born and starts yielding its fruit all the time.

In the words: 'The path of those on whom Thou hast bestowed Thy favors and blessings till we reach the goal'; there is an indication that Allâh has made the later generations similar to the former generations. When the souls of the later people, through perfect following and mutual temperamental affinities, are put in accord with the souls of the former, then grace descends from their hearts on the hearts of the later people and, when the recipient of the grace has established complete communion with the transmitter of grace and their accord reaches its limit, then the persons of both become one and they are lost in one another.

This is the condition which has been called the condition of union and at this stage the seeker is like the *Prophets, Saddaqîn, Shuhada and Salihîn* in heaven for he acquires a perfect resemblance with them in temperament and in essence. This is not unknown to the seers and scholars of sound and clear understanding.

**Eagerness and fervor are indispensable factors for the acceptance of prayer:** In *Surah Al-Fâtihah*, Allâh has taught such an excellent way of prayer that a better is not conceivable. It comprises all elements needed for stimulating heartfelt eagerness and fervor for prayer.

Eagerness and fervor are indispensable factors for the acceptance of prayer. A prayer that lacks fervor is mere verbal patter and not genuine prayer at all. At the same time, it is obvious that fervor in prayer is not at the command of a person at all times. Therefore it is of paramount importance that all the factors that generate fervor in the heart should be present in the mind of the supplicant at the time of prayer.

Every sensible person knows that there are only two incentives towards heart-felt enthusiasm.

**First**, the realization that Allâh is Perfect, Mighty and the embodiment of all excellences and that His mercy and His benevolence are indispensable for one's being and one's survival from beginning to end, and that He is the Source and Fountainhead of all grace.

**Second**, we are humble, weak and utterly dependent on His guidance and help.

These are the two incentives to fervor in prayer, and they are the perfect means for arousing enthusiasm for prayer. For, enthusiasm in prayer is induced only when one sees oneself utterly weak and hapless and in need of Divine help, and believes with firm faith that Allâh is the Almighty in the highest degree and the Lord of universal providence, Grace and Mercy and the Master of Requital. And that it is only in His power to provide for all human needs.

Accordingly in the beginning of *Surah Al-Fâtihah*, it is said that Allâh possesses all praiseworthy excellences and combines in Himself all attributes, and is the only One Who sustains all the worlds and is the Source of all mercies, and grants every one the fruits of his labor.

By enumerating these attributes, Allâh, the Most High, clearly sets forth that all power is in His hand, and all emanates from Him. He sets Himself forth as the Disposer of all the affairs of this world and the next, and the Cause of all causes, in relation to everything and the source of every benefit. Pointing out, at the same time, that independently of Him and His mercy, the life and comfort and tranquility of no sentient being is possible.

Next He instructed humanity to visualize: O Thou Fountainhead of all benevolence, we worship Thee alone and seek help from Thee alone as we are altogether humble and can do nothing on our own without the favor of Thy help and support.

Allâh, the Sublime, has thus furnished two incentives to prayer; first, His own Glory and its accompanying Compassion and Mercy, and secondly, the humility and unworthiness of a person. These are the two incentives that must be kept in mind at the time of prayer by the supplicants.

Those who have tasted some of the flavor of prayer know well that without these two incentives no true prayer can be offered and without them the fire of Divine love can scarcely burst into flame.

It is evident that one who does not keep in mind the Glory and Mercy and Perfect Power of the Almighty God-Allâh, can in no way turn to Allâh and that the soul of one who would not confess his own humbleness, helplessness and destitution, can never bend down before the Generous Lord.

This is a verity which does not call for any deep philosophy to be fully grasped. In fact, when the Magnificence of Allah and one's own humility and helplessness are borne in on mind, that particular condition itself convinces that it is the only approach to true prayer.

True worshippers appreciate well that the concept of these two aspects is essential for prayer; first, that Allâh has the power to grant every kind of providence and sustenance and mercy and reward and that His perfect attributes are ever-operative in their respective spheres and secondly, the conviction that a person can do nothing by himself, without Divine help and support.

**A haughty one falls down crying and hard-hearted one burst into tears:** Without doubt both these concepts are such that once they take hold of the heart and mind at the time of prayer, they transform suddenly the whole attitude of a person so much so that a haughty one falls down crying and a conceited and hard-hearted one bursts into tears.

This is the mechanism that quickens an indifferent corpse. Through the realization of these two factors, every heart is drawn towards prayer.

In brief, this is the spiritual means which turns the soul of a person towards Allâh and gives him an insight into his own weakness and the reality of Divine help. It is by this means that a person is transported to a state of self-forgetfulness, where no trace of his own opaque existence remains. And only the Majesty of Allâh the Fountainhead of every grace and mercy comes in sight.

Ultimately, through it, a state of obliteration-in-Allâh takes shape at the advent of which a person is bereft of all inclination towards any created being or towards his ego, or towards his volition, and is totally lost in the love of Allah. And through true perception his own entity and the entity of all created beings appears non-existent to him.

The All Mighty God - Allâh has called this state *Sirat al-mustaqîm-* the straight and the exact right path - to seek which He has taught the prayer: Lead us along the straight and right path till we reach the goal; meaning, Grant us the way of obliteration and Unity and Divine love which the above verses signify and cut us off totally from all others than Thee.

Thus in order to generate fervor in prayer, God, the Sublime, has provided such true incentives as transport the supplicant from the state of ego to that of self-forgetfulness and negation.

It should be remembered that *Surah Al-Fâtihah* is not just one of the ways of prayer for guidance; in fact, as we have shown, it is the most appropriate way to induce fervor and eagerness in the heart for prayer and which appeals to human nature as truly responsive to its urge.

The truth of the matter is that as Allâh has laid down laws in respect of other matters, so has been set down a particular way of prayer which comprises the incentives mentioned in *Surah Al-Fâtihah* and unless these two incentives are kept in mind not much enthusiasm can be aroused in prayer. The natural attitude in prayer is the one set down in *Surah Al-Fâtihah.* This then is one of the beauties of this *Surah* that it teaches prayer together with its incentives.

**_Surah Al-Fâtihah_ incorporates all the ingredients of Persuasiveness, in a beautiful manner:** A beauty of this *Surah* is that it has enumerated exhaustively, in every respect, the incentives towards the acceptance of guidance, for, perfect persuasiveness expressed in a cogent manner, is most effective. A special feature of the prayer contained in this Surah is that it appeals to the inner instincts of a human being in a perfectly natural manner.

There are two fundamental motives in human nature which prompt submission, viz., love and fear. Some people are touched by love, while others are moved by fear. The motive of love is certainly nobler but there may be-indeed there are people to whom love makes little or no appeal. They submit through fear of negative consequences of their actions.

In *Al-Fâtihah* an appeal has been made to both these human motives. First come those attributes of God which inspire love, "*Rabb* - the Creator, Sustainer and Guardian-Evolver to Perfection," "*Al-Rahmân* - the Most Gracious" and "*Al-Rahîm* the Ever Merciful." Then in their wake, as it were, follows the attribute, "*Mâlik e-Youmedîn* - Master of the Day of Requital", which reminds a person that if he does not mend his ways and does not respond to love and hope of a blessed reward, he should be prepared to render account of his deeds before God. ; Thus the motive' of fear based on the consequences of sinful actions is brought into play side by side with that of love, Mercy, Grace and blessed reward.

Nevertheless, we should remember that God's mercy far excels His displeasure, for it is implicit in the attribute of *'Mâlik e-Youmedîn'* that we are not appearing before a Judge but before a 'Supreme Master' Who has the power to forgive and Who will punish only where punishment is absolutely necessary.

## In terms of rational exposition perfect persuasiveness comprises three ingredients:

**First**, the inherent merits of the object towards which the persuasion is directed should be set out. This has been supplied in the words: Lead us along the path of integrity, rectitude and steadfastness which runs straight to the noble and virtuous goal. In these words the inherent quality of the way has been described, to induce enthusiasm for attainment to it.

**Second** ingredient of persuasiveness is that the benefits of the object of persuasion should be stated. This has-been done in the words: Lead us along the way by treading along with those who preceded us were rewarded and honored with Thy bounties. Thus by reference to those who succeeded by travelling along this path, Allâh generates enthusiasm for it.

**Third** ingredient of persuasiveness is to describe the privation and wretchedness of those who discard the object of persuasion. This has been done in the words: Safeguard us against the ways of those who abandoned the right path and took to other ways and incurred Divine displeasure and were lost. Thus He warned us against the harm that would befall in the event of deviating from the right path.

Thus *Surah Al-Fâtihah* incorporates all the ingredients of Persuasiveness, in a beautiful manner. It refers to the inherent qualities of the right path and to its benefits, and to the privation and wretchedness of those who abandon it.

**Its supplicatory clauses have been perfectly juxtaposed to the Divine attributes mentioned in the earlier part:** Another point of elegance in the *Surah* is that in addition to the highest standards of eloquence and fluency, its supplicatory clauses have been perfectly juxtaposed to the Divine attributes mentioned in the earlier part. Those practiced in the literary art appreciate how delicate this task is.

*Surah Al-Fâti<u>h</u>ah* first describes the four Divine attributes of grace. He is the Lord of universal Providence *(Rabb al 'Âlamîn)*, the Most Gracious *(Al-Ra<u>h</u>mân)*, the Ever Compassionate and Merciful *(Al-Ra<u>h</u>îm)*, Master of the Day of Requital *(Mâlik e-Youmedîn)*. Next the supplicatory expressions, rendering worship, seeking help, prayer, and begging favor have been juxtaposed to them, with such art that the expression having utmost correlation with an attribute is paired with it.

'We worship Thee alone' is juxtaposed to the Lord of universal Providence *(Rabb al - 'Âlamîn)* for the right to be worshipped originates in Providence and We worship Thee alone is thus befittingly and appropriately juxtaposed to it.

'We seek Thy guidance and help alone' is juxtaposed to *Al-Ra<u>h</u>mân* (the Most Gracious), for, Divine help, that is the capacity to worship Him, and the provision for all requirements, on which the welfare of the worshipper here and in the hereafter depends, do not represent the reward of any of his acts but are the manifestations of Graciousness, thus presenting a very close correlation between *Ra<u>h</u>mâniyyat* (Graciousness) and supplication for Divine help.

Similarly, the prayer: 'Lead us along the right path till we reach the goal'; is juxtaposed to *Al-Ra<u>h</u>îm* (the Ever

Merciful and Compassionate). For prayer is an effort and a striving and the reward that follows upon effort proceeds from the Divine attribute *Rahîmiyyat* (Mercy and Compassion).

Finally 'the path of those on whom You have bestowed (Your) blessings, not of those who incurred Your displeasure, nor of those who went astray'; is juxtaposed to 'Master of the Day of Requital *(Mâlik e-Youmiddîn)*, for requital pertains to the Master of the Day of Requital. Therefore, the juxtaposition of the supplication for bounty and for security against torment is appropriate to that attribute alone.

***Surah Al-Fâtihah* epitomizes all the objectives of the Holy Qur'ân:** Another beauty of *Surah Al-Fâtihah* is that it epitomizes all the objectives of the Holy Qur'ân. In other words, this *Surah* is a fine summary of the objectives of the Noble Qur'ân. It is to this that Allâh, the Most High, has referred in the Holy Quran: [115]

وَلَقَدْ آتَيْنَاكَ سَبْعًا مِنَ الْمَثَانِي وَالْقُرْآنَ الْعَظِيمَ (٨٧)

*And in fact We have given you the seven oft-recited (verses of Surah Al-Fâtihah) and the Grand Qur'ân. (15: 87)*

We have indeed bestowed on thee, O Prophet, the seven oft repeated verses of *Surah Al-Fâtihah* which comprehend briefly all the objectives of the Holy Qur'ân and have also granted thee the Great Qur'ân which expounds in detail all religious values.

[115] *The Holy Qur'ân: explained by 'Allamah Nooruddîn, rendered into English by Mrs. A. R. 'Omar; 'Abdul Mannân 'Omar*

That is why *Surah Al-Fâtihah* has been called the 'Mother of the Book' and the all-comprehensive *Surah.* It is the Mother of the Book in that all the objectives of the Holy Qur'ân can be gathered from it, and it is the all-comprehensive *Surah* because it comprehends in summary form all the branches of Qur'ânic sciences. It is because of this that the Holy Prophet Muhammad (peace and blessings of Allâh be on him) said that he who has read *Surah Al-Fâtihah*, has, in a manner, read the whole Qur'ân.

In short, Al-Fâtihah is a wonderful store-house of Qur'ânic knowledge. It is a short Chapter of seven brief verses, but it is a veritable mine of knowledge and wisdom. Aptly called "Mother of the Book," it is the very essence of the Holy Qur'an.

The teachings of the Grand Qur'ân and the Noble Prophet Muhammad صلى الله عليه وسلم is like the blessed light, let it shine on us! *Amîn.*

Made in the USA
Columbia, SC
23 January 2025

52304318R00114